CB
359
H5

Hillerbrand, Hans J.

Men and ideas in
the sixteenth century

D0885408

Lake Tahoe Community College
Learning Resources Center
So. Lake Tahoe, CA 95702

RAND McNALLY
EUROPEAN
HISTORY SERIES

MEN AND IDEAS IN THE SIXTEENTH CENTURY

HANS J. HILLERBRAND
City University of New York

24353

RAND McNALLY & COMPANY · Chicago

LAKE TAHOE COMMUNITY COLLEGE
LEARNING RESOURCES CENTER

INITIAL BOOKS IN
THE RAND McNALLY EUROPEAN HISTORY SERIES
George L. Mosse, advisory editor

GEORGE FASEL, Europe in Upheaval: The Revolutions of 1848
BRISON D. GOOCH, The Reign of Napoleon III
HANS J. HILLERBRAND, Men and Ideas in the Sixteenth Century
BARBARA JELAVICH, The Habsburg Empire in European Affairs,
    1814–1918
HARRY J. MAGOULIAS, Byzantine Christianity: Emperor, Church
    and the West
JOHN B. WOLF, Toward a European Balance of Power, 1620–1715

Copyright © 1969 by Rand McNally & Company
All rights reserved
Printed in the United States of America
Library of Congress Catalog Card Number 69:13297
Fourth Printing, 1971

To the memory of my brother Dieter Hillerbrand (1943-1968) whose promising career as a historian was cut short by a tragic accident.

Editor's Preface

It used to be thought that the sole object of history was to discover and set forth the facts. When the *English Historical Review* was founded it recommended such a procedure, for through it one "can usually escape the risk of giving offense." While much of this tradition has remained active in the teaching and writing of history, it has led, in turn, to a sharp reaction against such timidity and narrowness. History became a branch of philosophy or of the social sciences, and scholarship was in danger of being displaced by the search for general laws that might govern the development of all mankind. There is a hunger for history abroad in the land, but many of those who want to know about the past are rightly dissatisfied with arid narrations of fact (and turn to the historical novel instead), while others are bewildered by abstruse generalizations that seem to ignore the particular for the universal.

The books in the Rand McNally European History Series do not place themselves in either of these traditions. Instead, they recognize both the importance of accurate and detailed scholarship and the obligation to place such scholarship within a meaningful historical setting. They do not shun general ideas and assumptions; they test them in the crucible of research. This combination is always exciting, because it penetrates historical development; and this development, in each of its stages, illuminates a new dimension of mankind. A prominent historian once wrote, "What man is, only history tells."

Here "what man is" is told by scholars who have researched and reflected upon a significant period of history. They have taken this opportunity to present their conclusions in a manner that will attract and stimulate those who long for a lively account of the past. All of the authors in this series are specialists presenting their original insights, making it possible for all those interested in history to partake of their work.

George L. Mosse, *advisory editor*
Rand McNally European History Series

Preface

The intent of this modest volume is to sketch the main features of the Reformation of the sixteenth century. Both facts and interpretation are offered (it is hoped in an interesting synthesis) to propound the notion that the Reformation, while essentially religious in character, cannot be understood apart from its deep involvement in the larger affairs of European society at the time. While I have used the opportunity to present my own perspective on a number of events and men, I trust that I have not deviated too greatly from what might be called the scholarly consensus. And I should like to think that I have not deviated too much from scholarly competence either.

December 1968   H.J.H.
Durham, N.C.

Contents

Chapter 1

The History of Reformation History

The first comment to be made about the Reformation of the sixteenth century is that the history of Reformation scholarship during the past four hundred years is almost as exciting as the history of the period itself. But if almost as exciting, then also more discouraging. Bias and emotion have had a way of throwing their long shadows over the narratives of the period and often the writers do not seem to have talked about the same event. Take, for example, the following quotations from works on the Reformation published in recent years. The opinions of the writers concerning the man and the events they describe are somewhat at variance—to use a mild understatement.

> His [Luther's] was a deep, demanding soul, to whom no Catholic can in charity deny fraternal pity; but his mind contained also something of the devil, which made his arrogant desire to trace his own path turn to rebellion of the worst kind. . . . Luther certainly emerged battered, bruised and bleeding from the struggle with the Angel, but he failed to carry off real victory. He never obtained true peace of heart. And in the tragic battle which he fought during the whole of his life, almost everything at length slipped from his grasp. . . .
>
> It would be wrong to regard all those who were to support the

1

cause of heresy, even at the sacrifice of their own lives, as nothing but ambitious schemers. But the historian is sadly limited to the facts that are self-evident; and henceforth his account of the religious history of divided Christian Europe returns again and again to alliances, battles and treaties, rather than to theology, mysticism and spiritual adventure.

H. Daniel-Rops, *The Protestant Reformation*

Luther, as no one before him in more than a thousand years, sensed the import of the miracle of divine forgiveness. It is a miracle because there is no reason for it according to man's standards. . . .

The Reformation was a religious revival. Its attempt was to give man a new assurance in the presence of God and a new motivation in the moral life. How far it succeeded no one can ever tell. Nothing is so interior as faith.

R. H. Bainton, *The Reformation of the Sixteenth Century*

Medieval Christianity had been rich and varied, but it had been like a church where the furniture is cluttered, the altar obscured, and the corners undusted. The Reformation age, amid grievous destruction, swept away the clutter, pursued simplicity of vision, and directed the gaze of the worshipper towards that which truly mattered. After Luther it was not possible for either Protestant or Catholic to imitate some of the old ways of neglecting God's grace and sovereignty.

O. Chadwick, *The Reformation*

His [Luther's] rhetoric was heavy, vulgar, exaggerated, repetitious, for he wrote or spoke hastily on the spur of the moment or in the grasp of passion. Vain and jealous, he easily yielded to flattery. . . . He forged papal documents and misrepresented Catholic doctrine. . . . Mentally he was brilliant, but superficial: a frenzied student, he later abandoned profound study and coasted easily on ready eloquence.

N. C. Eberhardt, *A Summary of Catholic History*

To put the matter another way: the Reformation is an illustration *par excellence* for the pervading influence of value judgments on historical writing. During the past four hundred years the historians of the Reformation have virtually had an armory of axes to grind—and the result has been all too obvious and rather painful for all those who feel that history can be written "as it actually happened" to use the phrase made famous by Ranke.

The eminent characteristic of Reformation scholarship from the sixteenth century onward has been its staunchly confessional orientation. The narratives were written *ad majorem Dei gloriam,* though exactly what was "God's greater glory" was defined differently by Catholics and Protestants, both lengthily quoting sources (including the Bible!) in support of their particular positions. Epithets flew hither and thither, with each side loath to be outdone by the other. Catholics saw Luther and the other Protestant reformers as immoral men and ignorant theologians, while the Protestants, lacking personalities on the Catholic side of the fence on which to bestow such compliments, used equally bold language to describe the state of the Catholic Church on the eve of the Reformation as immoral, corrupt, and unbiblical.

Moreover, the assessments of the consequences of the Reformation differed drastically on both sides. Catholics saw the Reformation as the great cause of the secularization of the West, while Protestants hailed it as the dawn of the modern world. Thus, the eminent political theorist, Joseph de Maistre, writing early in the nineteenth century was persuaded that the connections between the Reformation and the French Revolution were many (and evil),' while Lord Acton concluded that the Reformation had been a milestone in the progress toward human freedom.

A great leap forward in the understanding of the Reformation was made by the German historian Leopold von Ranke, whose monumental *German History in the Age of the Reformation,* first published in 1839, found sufficient coherence in the early sixteenth century to see it as a historical epoch even though he primarily concerned himself, as the title of his work indicated, with the German course of events. More than that, Ranke, a Lutheran whose religious views were important in the formation of his historical ideas, made a significant contribution to Reformation historiography by insisting—in line with his famous and often quoted postulate that history must be written *wie es gewesen ist* ("as it actually happened")—on an extensive use of primary sources *and* their critical verification: sources had been cited before, sometimes volumes of them, but rather without critical acumen. Ranke's rich and colorful canvas depicted a society that was affected as much by political events as it was by religious ones. Indeed, he emphasized the interrelation of politics and religion as the eminent characteristic of the age. Perhaps his greatest significance for Reformation studies lay in this assertion, which entailed a great stress on a politically oriented understanding of the sixteenth century. Much of Reformation scholarship since Ranke has followed this lead.

Ranke's stress on the exact and critical use of sources, coming as it did at a time of an increasing sophistication of historical methodology, helped bring about a vast publication of source materials in all areas and aspects of the sixteenth century. Many of these publications have to do with theology. Virtually all the writings of Luther, Zwingli, and Calvin, for example, were made available in scholarly editions. At the same time, editions of government sources were published. Thus, the materials pertaining to several important German diets in the sixteenth century, as well as similar sources for other countries, have been edited.

If Ranke can be said to have signified the political (or diplomatic) approach to the Reformation era (alongside of which the old ecclesiastical approach continued), another group of scholars relegated the political as well as the religious issues into the background—somewhat in line with Voltaire's remark that the monkish squabble "in a corner of Saxony" brought nothing but "discord, fury, and misfortune." Whatever significance was attributed to the age was seen in areas other than religion. These scholars, notably Wilhelm Dilthey, busied themselves with the social, cultural, and economic aspects of the sixteenth century and saw the eminent characteristic of the time best expressed by the term Renaissance. To them the real issues of the age were the non-religious ones: the secularization of society, the social upheavals, the economic developments, the cultural consequences of the Reformation.

If these were, broadly speaking, the main lines of interpretation in the past, the question arises as to what interpretations and schools of thought can be discerned today. Much progress has been made, much common ground exists, but no general consensus prevails and divergent perspectives continue to characterize the scholarly scene. Three of these may be distinguished. We shall call them the ecclesiastical, the secular, and the Marxist.

One group of scholars continues to view the age of the Reformation from an ecclesiastical and religious vantage point. Here the centrality of the religious turmoil is stressed, the only difference being that Protestants still see it positively while Catholics view it negatively. The former note the renewal of apostolic teaching or authentic Christian piety, the latter emphasize the revolution against centuries of Christian tradition. Accordingly, the canvas is covered with intense colors. The state of the Catholic Church on the eve of the Reformation, the theological incisiveness of the Protestant reformers, the cultural consequences of the Protestant Reformation—these are issues where the assessments on both sides differ greatly.

While this traditional picture is still accurate even today, a dramatic change has been taking place among Catholic Reformation scholars during the past few years, a change that may well be considered the most significant development in Reformation studies. It had its first and epoch-making manifestation in the publication of Joseph Lortz's *Die Reformation in Deutschland* (1939), in which this distinguished Catholic historian produced a vastly different assessment of Luther and the Protestant Reformation than had theretofore been the case among Catholics. Lortz sought to understand the historical necessity for the Reformation by noting the deplorable state of Catholic theology in the early sixteenth century due to the influence of William of Occam. Luther was heir to a theologically confusing situation and his dissent was understandable. What is more, he was a religious genius and his theology voiced in many ways authentic biblical insights. But his fatal error was that he was not, as Lortz put it, "a full listener". In other words, he did not consider all of Scripture, but only a part, and he did, moreover, place his own views over those of the church. Luther, according to Lortz, was too subjective.

One can hardly overestimate the significance of Lortz's work, which has heralded a new type of Catholic Reformation studies. In the English language John M. Todd's *Martin Luther* (1964) or John Dolan's *A History of the Reformation: A Conciliatory Assessment of Conflicting Views* (1965) might be singled out, the latter denoting in its title its conciliatory and irenic spirit.

A second stream of contemporary Reformation scholarship is characterized by what might be called the secular approach. This clumsy and awkward label suggests the stress on a variety of cultural or political emphases as the significant aspects of the sixteenth century on the part of some scholars. These writers do not consider the ecclesiastical happenings as crucially important and consequently say little about them. They find the true significance of the age to lie in the emergence of the modern nation state, the geographic discoveries, or the intellectual currents associated with the terms Humanism or

Renaissance. A comprehensive statement of this approach has come from the Dutch historian Enno van Gelder in *The Two Reformations of the Sixteenth Century* (1961), which contrasts the Protestant Reformation with a larger reformatory development, exemplified by Erasmus, Montaigne, and others, and holds the latter to have been of greater importance.

There is, finally, the economic interpretation of the Reformation. Its presupposition is the principle of economic determinism and its basic contention is that the upheaval of the sixteenth century, including the religious one, was essentially economic in character. The most sophisticated version is the Marxist one, which views the time as a revolution of the early bourgeoisie against the feudal order, and was most pronounced, therefore, in the cities where the old order was dramatically crumbling. The presence of religious and theological controversies is not denied, though these are seen as the outgrowth of more basic economic or social issues. Thus, the failure of Luther and Zwingli to reach agreement concerning the Lord's Supper was not due to theological differences, but to the rejection by German Protestants of Zwingli's political anti-Hapsburg policies. The real hero of the drama is Thomas Müntzer, whose theological affirmations are seen as but a veneer covering his more intense concern for the social aspirations of the common people.

A less sophisticated economic interpretation (though, perhaps, one more widely held) suggests that the various ecclesiastical changes in the sixteenth century and the concomitant rejection of Catholicism were primarily attributable to the greed of rulers, city councils, and the nobility who coveted the wealth of the church, or resented its legal and political influence, and simply used religious or theological rationalizations to cover up their real purposes.

We cannot adjudge here the strengths and weaknesses of these three divergent approaches to the religious turmoil in the sixteenth century, though they are present in all three. The religious historian seems to be a bit too exuberant at times in his assessment of the intensity of religious conviction, but rightly sees that religion did play an important role in the course of events; the political and economic historians in turn are right not only in pointing to important political, economic, and cultural developments, but also in perceiving that not all who cried "Religion, religion" in the sixteenth century meant what they said. Perhaps the crux of the matter is balance—the willingness to acknowledge the complexity of events and men, the courage to

defy simple labels and easy generalizations. The striking reorientation of Catholic Reformation scholarship, to which we have referred,
shows that this is possible. Lines, once considered rigid and immovable, have become flexible; interpretations, once utterly at odds, have
been considerably harmonized.

If the intensification of this trend is the most obvious desideratum
of Reformation scholarship, a second (and related) one is surely the
intensification of a strictly historical preoccupation with the era. This
may be a strange comment to make, but the point is that we know
far too little about the actual historical details of the ecclesiastical
transformation in the early years of the Reformation, the attitudes of
clergy, burghers, nobility, artisans, and so on to the Lutheran proclamation. Likewise, the social and economic conditions in areas of
Protestant success remain enigmatic. And the policies of Philipp of
Hesse, of Moritz of Saxony, or the history of the League of Schmalkald,
are far from being adequately assessed. What is true with regard to
the German examples just cited is equally applicable elsewhere in
Europe. Only recently has attention been called to the significance of
Thomas Cromwell and the influence of administrative changes in English government on the ecclesiastical transformation in England.

This stress on a historical approach entails two consequences. For
one, it would clear the veil of ignorance that hangs over many of the
strictly historical events and developments in the sixteenth century.
For another, it would place the theological as well as the church-his-
torical course of events in a broader setting and would allow more
adequate consideration of the relation of the ecclesiastical transformation to certain political, cultural, and economic features of the time.
For example, we are only beginning to understand the role played by
the nobility in various countries in the introduction of the Protestant
Reformation, even as we have no more than preliminary generalizations on the relation of humanism to the Reformation.

Such an approach would seek to understand the sixteenth century in
a more synoptic fashion than has heretofore often been the case. Lord
Acton's famous exhortation to study problems, not periods, can surely
be modified to mean that with respect to the Reformation the most
illuminating insights will be obtained by a study of the European
development as a whole rather than by a restriction to national histories. Traditionally, most histories of the Reformation have placed the
course of events in Germany in the forefront of their attention, rele-
gating the development in France, England, and other countries to the

background. This kind of geographic parochialism is unfortunate, for numerous parallels existed—the political and even economic setting, such specific issues as the disposal of ecclesiastical property, the role of the monks, the import of the ruler, etc.—to warrant not only a broad purview but also the drawing of lines from one to the other for the purpose of better understanding both.

The accomplishments of Reformation scholarship have been extensive and remarkable; still, much remains to be done. The pages that follow here are a progress report. They point out scholarly progress and underscore the need for future work. For those disciples of Clio who are fascinated by the interplay of a variety of factors and forces in the affairs of men and nations, the Reformation era is a magnificent area of endeavor.

Chapter 2

Before the Storm

The most enticing approach to the Reformation is to find its clue in the conditions prevailing in early sixteenth-century society. Most of the schools of Reformation historiography mentioned in the first chapter seem to agree on this point: Marxists note the dramatic economic changes of the time; Protestants paint a dreary picture of ecclesiastical abuse and perversion; Catholics admit that much in the church stood in need of correction. In short, attention is generally called to a variety of political and intellectual changes in fifteenth-century Europe and the suggestion made that these provide the clues for the Reformation. Somehow or other, so the argument runs, the time was ripe for ecclesiastical reform, Europe was crying for a Reformation, and an upheaval of sorts would have occurred even if Martin Luther had died in the cradle. None other than Leopold von Ranke wrote in the beginning of his famous *Reformation History* with a bothersome flair for abstract language (not uncommon among continental writers), "When the times are accomplished, higher aspirations and more enlightened schemes spring up out of the tottering remains of institutions, which they utterly overthrow and efface: for so God works in the world."

This scholarly consensus directs us to the time before the controversy. But this is easier said than done, for to assess the temper of the time, particularly as it affected religion and the church, is difficult

9

indeed. What was the state of the church? What was the intensity of religious devotion among the people? Were the people restless, discontent, dissatisfied about their religion? Did they yearn for ecclesiastical renewal? Or were they content with the religious status quo—as much, or as little, as people always had been? Moreover, what political, economic, or intellectual developments had a bearing on ecclesiastical events? These questions must be satisfactorily answered or the problem of the relation of the state of society in the early sixteenth century to the Protestant Reformation remains unsolved.

Unfortunately, our knowledge of ecclesiastical affairs at the time is still quite limited and thus any comment made must be considered tentative. Only the main features of the ecclesiastical landscape have been established. They depict a rich ecclesiastical life and a preoccupation with religious matters on the part of the people. The evidence seems impressive, even though it focuses on externals, and spirituality is somewhat difficult to ascertain from the outside. There was extensive religious instruction. Sermons were frequently preached and devotional books widely printed. It is said that more than half of all books printed between the time of the invention of movable type and the outbreak of the Reformation dealt with religion. Even the Bible was partially available in various European languages.

Men took their religious obligations seriously. Recent researches have indicated the extent to which bequests were made to religious causes; contributions to ecclesiastical and religious causes were frequent and liberal. Thus, Professor W. K. Jordan, maintaining that wills were "mirrors of men's souls as truly as they were mirrors of their mundane aspirations," has shown that £29,907 were given for religious purposes in England during 1480-90, and £46,615 between 1521 and 1530. The increasing prominence of indulgences in the latter part of the fifteenth century is an additional case in point (they would not have been so successful had the people not been willing to purchase them) as is the extensive preoccupation with saints and relics noted by so many contemporaries.

There were other features. The movement of the so-called Modern Devotion indicated the presence of a lively spirituality in Holland and Northwest Germany. The "Brethren of the Common Life," as the followers of the Modern Devotion were known, lived together without formal vows and sought to live their piety by performing works of Christian charity. They preached, fed the hungry, housed those in need, and educated the young. Pope Adrian VI, Luther, and Erasmus were three early sixteenth-century figures who came into contact with the Brethren—the one a pope, the other a heretic, and the third of dubious orthodoxy! Obviously, the consequences of the Modern Devotion could be quite ambiguous. The striking earthiness that characterized the theological reflection of the Brethren of the Common Life is best expressed perhaps in their own *Imitation of Christ,* that famous devotional classic. Whether they were theologically orthodox has been debated. Even if they were not, this would be less important than their demonstration of the presence of spiritual vitality within the Catholic Church.

Parallels existed elsewhere in Europe. In Italy the Oratories of the Divine Love sought to revive the Church by the practice of piety, and in Spain Cardinal Francisco Jiménez de Cisneros worked long and hard to remove ecclesiastical abuses and to instill new spiritual vigor into the church. In England the humanist and reformer John Colet appealed for authentic spirituality in the church. And in Germany, France, and elsewhere conscientious bishops, whose names history has forgotten, sought to be good churchmen and improve ecclesiastical life within the confines of their responsibilities.

This takes us to one aspect of the early sixteenth-century scene that stood in self-conscious aloofness from the main theological tradition of the time: Christian humanism that, nurtured by classical antiquity and Christianity alike, offered an alternative to the somewhat arid scholasticism of the fifteenth century. The members of the phenomenon subsumed under this heading were rather heterogeneous in their orientation and one may well raise the question whether the generic heading is proper at all. For the sake of convenience one may suggest, however, that despite variations in individual emphasis, a common denominator characterized certain men who somehow or other strove for a synthesis of Christian teachings and classical thought. They were indebted to the Italian humanist tradition that, ever since Petrarch, had offered new and dynamic approaches first to the language and literature of classical antiquity, then to its history and philosophy as well. They gloried in the classical style of life and their call *ad fontes* was an exhortation to authentic and firsthand, rather than secondhand, acquaintance with the literary monuments (and thereby the thought) of antiquity.

These Christian humanists owed a major debt to Erasmus, whose eminent contribution it was to have fused classical antiquity with the Christian gospel. To describe the Christian religion, Erasmus used the expression *philosophia Christi* ("the philosophy of Christ") and while his understanding of it was not devoid of strictly theological emphases, it did stress what we might call the practical side of Christianity, pointing out that Jesus' teaching was based on meekness, patience, and the rejection of the temporal. Erasmus was an aesthete, an aristocrat of the mind, and consequently he had little empathy for either the earthy forms of religion rampant among the people or the temporal preoccupations of the church. Still, he never outrightly questioned the teaching of the church and surely meant to be its loyal son, even though his way of theologizing was different from that pursued by other theologians and churchmen. The notion (noted right away by contemporaries) that he laid the egg that Luther subsequently hatched, showed that it was not difficult to relate his teaching to that of Luther.

Even more significant—and paradigmatic for the orientation of Christian humanism as a whole—was Erasmus' preoccupation with the early Fathers of the Christian Church and his concomitant emphasis on the linguistic tools necessary for studying the Fathers and Scripture. Erasmus published works of numerous Fathers, Ambrose, Augustine, Basil, Cyprian, Hilary, Irenaeus, Jerome, John Chrysostom, to name but a few, and thereby confronted his contemporaries with a type of theological reflection they were not very familiar with. In 1516 he published his *magnum opus,* the New Testament in Greek. The implication of this publication was that the Latin Vulgate did not really provide the authentic text and that in order to understand the New Testament one must go to its original language. In 1505 Erasmus had published Lorenzo Valla's *Annotations on the New Testament,* which propounded essentially the same argument, namely, that the Latin version was not as accurate as the original Greek. His stress on the Greek text entailed not only the minute analysis of the New Testament language—the original meaning of the words—but also made the knowledge of Greek important for the whole theological enterprise.

Alongside Erasmus were other Christian humanists whose literary contribution aided in the emergence of a new approach to understanding the New Testament and the Bible. In France it was Jacques Lefèvre, also called Faber Stapulensis, whose biblical commentaries, especially the one on the Book of Romans, showed the fruitful emphases and insights that the new approach rendered. In England, John Colet lectured on the Pauline Epistles, utilizing his competence in Greek, and in Germany, John Reuchlin pointed to the importance of

Hebrew for the understanding of the Old Testament. Reuchlin's insistence that the writings of Jewish scholars were indispensable for an authentic approach to the Old Testament led him into serious controversy. The *Letters of Obscure Men,* published in 1515, was a devastating satire on the narrow-mindedness of the traditional theologians who spent their time in theological hairsplitting and despised everything that was new.

None of these Christian humanists was an ardent reformer nor did any one of them propound his understanding of the nature of the Christian religion in conscious opposition to the Catholic Church. That they pursued a different approach, however, was unmistakable. Thereby they added both to the liveliness and to the confusion of the theological scene.

The Catholic Church was by no means bereft of genuine spirituality, of sensitive churchmen, or of concern for ecclesiastical vigor. On the other hand, we must not assume that all was exuberant bliss—a notion that would be historically inaccurate (and probably biblically erroneous as well). It would be inaccurate, since contrary evidence is not difficult to find. It would be erroneous, since it would overlook that the Christian Church at no time in its long history, both before and after the sixteenth century, has ever fully realized the biblical ideal to which it aspires. The notion of *ecclesia reformanda* ("the church must ever be reformed") is a timeless commentary upon the history of the Christian Church. Sensitive churchmen, no matter of what time or place, have bewailed the perennial deviation from the ideal and the lack of spirituality. Some may have been excessively sensitive in this regard, while others surely had substance in fact with their "attack upon Christendom"—to use Sören Kierkegaard's phrase. In short, the real has not always been identical with the ideal in Christian history, neither in actual fact nor in the frank admission of the faithful.

It is with this in mind that we must listen to the cries of the critics and assess the profferred evidence of religious pervasion in the early sixteenth century. That there were critics—from Erasmus on down— is well known and must not be belabored. And that their charges had some substance in fact seems also clear enough. The evidence is available. Some of it comes from private pamphleteers, from noisy critics who were persuaded that the church was embarked upon a fatal collision course. Some evidence comes from official lists of grievances, the *gravamina,* compiled periodically in Germany by the temporal authorities to express formal dissatisfaction with the state of the church.

Other evidence comes from visitation records (the records of routine examinations of clergy by their superiors), sermons, and contemporary descriptions of society.

The foci of dissatisfaction with the church seem to have been two. One pertained strictly to the church and singled out the immorality of the clergy, the frequency of clerical absenteeism, and the low level of clerical competence as the major ills. The other pertained more generally to the place of the church in society—the traditional legal prerogatives of the hierarchy or the excessive financial demands of the church. In both respects the dissatisfaction obviously had a basis in fact. The cleric who dressed in the latest fashion or who frequented the local tavern was not merely a fabrication in the imaginative mind of muckraking social critics. How many of them there were, however, is another question. Reports of violations of the vow of celibacy were not infrequent, both in official documents and the criticism of contemporaries. But again the question is not so much the existence of such demeanor, but its frequency and its impact upon the public mind. What evidence there is suggests that only a small minority of clerics were cited for violations. On the other hand, there is no doubt that the foibles of many a parson, whose mortification of the flesh did not include celibacy, never gained public attention. Thus, the actual situation may well have been worse than the fragmentary evidence supports. But even this cannot drastically alter the general fact that we are dealing with exceptions rather than the rule. One must remember that *only* violations of the regulations found their way into the visitation records or the observations of contemporaries. To arrive at conclusions concerning the characteristics of the time on such a basis is highly precarious. The conscientious cleric, who devoutly carried out his priestly functions, the spiritually minded monks—these remained nameless, but were, by all odds, more typical than the exception dramatized by vociferous critics. Early sixteenth-century accounts of ecclesiastical life lengthily recorded the piety of the people and the vitality of the church. If all this is too confusing, a modern parallel might well be noted here. How should we assess a contemporary situation? If our only source of information about mid-twentieth-century Catholicism were the "Letters from the Vatican" published by Xavier Rynne in *The New Yorker*, with all their revelling in curial intrigue, we surely would be inadequately informed. A faithful Catholic would tell us quite a different story.

At this point a word must be said about the Renaissance papacy, that motley group of pontiffs who occupied the throne of St. Peter during the latter half of the fifteenth century. Even Catholics will not dissent from the statement that these popes represented a low ebb in the history of the Roman see and that men like Alexander VI or Julius II hardly were paragons of spirituality. Rather, these popes aspired to transform Rome into a center of culture and learning: thus, Nicolaus V founded the Vatican Library and Sixtus IV built the magnificent chapel named in his honor. More than that, however, most of these popes, who were scions of eminent Italian families, worked to increase the place of their families in Italian political affairs. As a result the curia increasingly became but another secular Italian court, guided by men who were primarily Renaissance figures and Italian statesmen. Since fifteenth-century Italian politics were frequently taken straight out of Machiavelli, with poison, intrigue, murder, and all the rest, such papal involvement did not make for model deportment.

In short, on the eve of the Reformation the papacy was by no means a lively spiritual institution. Consequently, the conclusion is drawn that this state of affairs was of major significance for the Protestant Reformation. But, no matter how persuasive, the argument is not completely accurate. The crucial question is how much knowledge of the papal demeanor in the second half of the fifteenth century actually filtered down to the man-in-the-street throughout Europe. To answer is difficult. Diaries of Roman citizens from that time are remarkably silent on this point. The historian, who by prying into archives or reading secret correspondence is in a far more knowledgeable position than were the contemporaries, can make no more fatal error than assume that what he has garnered in the way of information and facts was general knowledge at the time. Accordingly, we must not overestimate the import of the admittedly deplorable papal state of affairs for subsequent Reformation events—except, perhaps, to say the obvious: when the storm broke loose the curia seems to have lacked that fulness of spiritual sensitivity that might have led to different approaches to the problems engendered by the Wittenberg professor. In all this, the historian knows that men's opinions and convictions are produced by rumors no less than facts: even if the true conditions in the curia were not public knowledge, wild rumors may well have led to the same result as would have facts.

The misgivings on the part of many concerning the place of the church in society, on the other hand, were a more serious matter. The hand of the church lay upon society in numerous ways. Over the centuries the church had garnered rights, privileges, and prerogatives in economic and legal affairs which made for wealth and power. This was increasingly resented, especially since society was changing while the church seemed an immovable island in a sea of change.

This made for almost constant tensions between the church and the secular authorities over these traditional financial and legal rights of the church. Evidence for numerous lawsuits between individuals and the church over these matters is not hard to come by. One of the most famous cases was that of the London merchant Richard Hunne, who on the death of his infant son in 1514 refused to pay the customary fee to the cleric for the burial. By the early sixteenth century people had become quite critical of the place of the church in the society and gave occasional evidence that they were determined to change it.

Actually, it was changed in a number of ways. The increasing accumulation of power in the hands of the ruler also meant increased authority over the external affairs of the church. The trend toward national churches whose external affairs were largely controlled by the political authorities was one of the most characteristic features of the fifteenth century. As early as 1324 Marsiglio of Padua had sketched in his *Defensor Pacis* the picture of a national church independent of Rome. In France the Pragmatic Sanction of Bourges (1438) entrusted the French king with considerable power over the French church. And even though the Sanction came to be the cause of a constant tug-of-war between the papacy and the French crown, the Concordat of Bologna, which at long last ended this situation in 1516, did not essentially diminish the voice of the king in the external affairs of the French church.

A similar situation prevailed in England and Spain where appointments to positions of ecclesiastical eminence and matters of church finance were virtually controlled by the king. Only the German Empire, with its absence of a strong central authority, showed a different picture, though it must be said that most territorial rulers successfully imitated, within the modest confines of their domains, the example of the great monarchies in the West. One widely cited saying of the time was *Dux Cliviae est papa in terris suis* ("The Duke of Cleves is pope in his territory") and it seems to have expressed generally held sentiment.

European society was generally in a state of dynamic flux and transition. In the realm of politics, rulers struggled for increasing power over the nobility and in the main they were successful. In the cities, especially in Germany, a new class of burghers emerged, determined to take their place in society, exhibiting interests not identical with those of either the nobility or the commoners. The peasants, finally, were at the bottom of society, a bit bewildered over what was going on around them, their chronic restlessness and periodic uprisings in the decades prior to 1517 revealing their temper of discontent.

In short, ecclesiastical life in the early sixteenth century was varied and complex. Spirituality and corruption stood side by side. Ecclesiastical reform was demanded by some and abuses were denounced by others. Still, to see European Christendom on the eve of the Reformation as a restless giant seething with a deep yearning for reform, as a sort of ecclesiastical pressure cooker with the heat turned on, seems erroneous and certainly not supported by any kind of ironclad evidence. The restlessness abroad in the years before the Reformation pertained more to the legal and financial implications of the place of the church in society than to the zeal for either a theological reorientation or a correction of prevailing ecclesiastical abuses. In particular, the zeal for theological reorientation was hardly widespread. Yet precisely this constituted the characteristic mark of the early Reformation, which did not stress the ecclesiastical corruption but argued a theological case that would have been just as valid four hundred years earlier.

To be sure, when all was said and done, there were various willing handmaidens of the Protestant cause. John Foxe, the sixteenth-century English martyrologist and chronicler, went to great lengths to single out printing as one and his point is well taken. Without the printed page the reformers would never have been able to spread their message.

With the insight of hindsight it is not difficult to discern how conditions in the early sixteenth century constituted a congenial setting for the spread of those ideas we have come to label Protestant. No doubt Europe and the Catholic Church would still have been different in 1550, compared with 1517, had Luther, Zwingli, or Calvin not survived infancy. To deny this runs counter to the dynamic quality of society and the genius of the Catholic Church to find within itself the resources for renewal and reform.

But such an acknowledgment must not lead to the conclusion that an ecclesiastical storm hung in the air. To accept the reality of change and the dynamic atmosphere in the early sixteenth century is not to accept the inevitability of revolutionary upheaval. In 1517 almost anything might have happened: slow or dramatic ecclesiastical reform, widespread dissent or sporadic heresy. What did happen and began to engage the attention of men everywhere during the next several years was certainly not what should have been anticipated. An obscure professor of theology raised several theological questions: he neither denounced the immorality of the clergy nor the usurpation of judicial rights by the hierarchy, but presented a positive picture of what to him was the essence of the Christian faith.

Specifically with respect to Germany, the constitutional situation played an important role in the advance of Luther's teaching. To call it an indispensable prerequisite for the success of the Reformation is hardly an overstatement, for had Luther been born a Frenchman or an Englishman, his fate (and that of his cause) would have been different. As a matter of fact, the case can be put even more tellingly: Had Luther taught fifty miles to the south at Leipzig and been a subject of the rabidly Catholic Duke George of Saxony, he would not have seen the success of his Reformation or the establishment of a new Christian tradition. The absence of a strong central authority in the Empire, together with the benevolent attitude of Luther's territorial ruler, allowed the new theology to gain a foothold and consolidate its successes before serious opposition set in. In England or France the authorities would have moved more swiftly, giving the new heresy little chance for breath.

If we say that in 1517 the time was ripe for Martin Luther and his reformatory message—and this we must not deny—we must add that it continued to be ripe in 1518 and several years afterward. The congeniality of the time to reform, its anti-clericalism, its criticism of ecclesiastical abuses, and the other aspects mentioned, would have made little difference, for example, if the Saxon Elector had arrested Luther in 1518 as the curia persuaded him to do, if Emperor Maximilian had not died in 1519, if his successor had been Francis rather than Charles V, if the Turks had not been a nagging threat to Western Christendom during the crucial years of ecclesiastical transformation—to cite only a few 'ifs'. All these factors proved to be important. They made for the success of the Reformation which accordingly, in the final analysis, was based on reasons that went beyond the temper of the first decade of the sixteenth century. And success is, after all, what counts in history. Narratives of abortive movements may be exciting;

they are rarely important. The success of the Reformation must be sought in factors other than the temper of the time.

We must be careful, in sum, not to think of dynamic and unstable European society on the eve of the Reformation in such a way as to make a revolutionary turmoil, such as came with the Protestant Reformation, an inevitable consequence. No matter how pregnant with change, the time was not inevitably steering toward revolution. What this means is that Europe stumbled, as it were, into the ecclesiastical transformation we have come to call Reformation, even as that obscure professor of theology, Martin Luther, who precipitated it, stumbled into the indulgences controversy.

Chapter 3

Conspicuous Beginnings

Time-honored sentiment clothes the beginnings of the Reformation in a dramatic setting: the hammering of ninety-five theses on the door of the Wittenberg Castle Church by Martin Luther, professor of biblical studies at the university there, who had become incensed over what seemed to him a blatantly unspiritual sale of indulgences in the vicinity of Wittenberg. The point is well taken, for Luther's theses precipitated a vigorous controversy that soon became the cause célèbre of the theological world. Initially, the focus of attention was the problem of indulgences and other peripheral theological issues. After he had recovered from his astonishment over the notoriety of his theses, Luther explained his position in several pamphlets, found supporters, notably his colleague on the Wittenberg faculty, Andreas Bodenstein Carlstadt, but also encountered eminent antagonists, above all John Eck, of the University of Ingolstadt, who pursued him with relentless theological anger.

The controversy shifted quickly to more basic theological concerns, until it centered in the problem of the place of the papacy within the church and of the locus of religious authority. Luther increasingly showed himself out of step with his fellow theologians as he continued to insist upon being convinced by scriptural reasoning rather than submitting to ecclesiastical fiat. Scholarship has not completely resolved the question of how far Luther's theological reformulation had proceeded by 1517 when the indulgences controversy broke out. Even if he still was a good Catholic in those days, as has been suggested, he underwent a rapid and incisive change during the months of vehement theological debate in 1518 and 1519. This can be shown in a number of ways. For example, an elaborate explanation of his ninety-five theses written in the spring of 1518, entitled *Resolutions*, disclosed that his thought still wavered between Scripture and tradition as the norm for authority, between acceptance of the pope and his rejection. But by 1519 this uncertainty had truly been resolved, at least in part, by his affirmation of Scripture over tradition.

Luther's quest for theological clarification reached its initial climax in the spring of 1519 when he and his colleague Carlstadt met the staunch Catholic protagonist at Leipzig for a debate. The range and depth of points covered on that occasion between Eck and Carlstadt was impressive. Luther, however, stole the show—and this not so much because of his theological profundity or elaborate competence in patristic or medieval authorities, but because of his assertion that certain decisions of the Council of Constance indicated that councils can be in error. Accordingly, even a general council is not an infallible norm of faith. Luther could hardly have made a more dramatic statement; Duke George of Saxon, who was present, uttered the German equivalent of "I'll be damned" and left the room. No doubt a revolutionary affirmation had been made by Luther. With the papacy *and* church councils rejected as authorities, what was left? At Leipzig Luther made it clear that for him the final court of appeal was neither pope nor council, but Scripture.

From then on it was a matter of time before the inevitable. As matters turned out, however, another year passed before the Roman curia rallied to action and pronounced the verdict: the bull *Exsurge Domine* of June 1520 declared forty-one statements of Luther's to be heretical and called on him to revoke them.

The papal bull sought not only to settle the theological controversy that had dominated the attention of the theologians since Luther's ninety-five theses, but also to conclude the development that had paralleled this controversy from the very beginning, namely, the official ecclesiastical proceedings against Luther. Begun with astounding speed in December 1517 with Albert of Hohenzollern's report of Luther's theses to Rome, they had gained momentum the following year when the curia sought to have Luther arrested as a suspected heretic.

Things were a bit confusing that summer and from this distance it is not altogether clear if the curia had second thoughts about such rapid procedure or if the intervention of Luther's ruler, Elector Frederick of Saxony, eventually saved the day. At any rate, Luther was neither arrested nor did he have to appear at Rome. He was examined at Augsburg in October 1518 by one of the most erudite men of the curia, Cardinal Cajetan. The encounter was fruitless since Luther refused to recant; it was exasperating since both men argued along different lines. Cajetan cited a host of ecclesiastical statements, while Luther pleaded to be persuaded with scriptural argumentation.

At that juncture political considerations delayed the action of the curia. The grave illness and subsequent death in January 1519 of the German Emperor Maximilian I and the ensuing negotiations concerning the election of a successor occupied the attention of the curia and relegated the case of the Wittenberg professor temporarily to the background. Moreover, since Luther's ruler, Frederick, as one of the German electors, occupied a crucial role in the election, the curia could ill afford to force an issue that would alienate him. Such was bound to happen if Luther's case were pursued, for Frederick had shown himself unwilling to become a partner of any hasty and thus possibly unfair resolution of the matter.

All the while Luther remained filially submissive to the church and the pope. He had stumbled into the controversy and was both shocked and perturbed over its growing dimension. Nothing was further from his mind than to incite an ecclesiastical revolution or to precipitate widespread reform. His spiritual pilgrimage had taken him to a new interpretation of the Christian faith and what he meant to do in his numerous tracts was merely to describe this new interpretation and point to its various ramifications. Clearly, he meant to pursue his theological insight within the church.

The problem was that some of the men on the other side of the fence, notably John Eck and Sylvester Prierias, were dogmatic divines who pursued their theological antagonist with relentless vigor and determination. Astute theologians that they were, they sensed the theologically questionable character of some of Luther's pronouncements and their attack upon him was both devastating and comprehensive. In so doing, they overlooked the religious intensity of Luther's proclamation and the fact that Luther, above all, wanted his religion taken seriously. He wanted inward spirituality rather than the performance of externals, dependence on God and his grace rather than on man and his autonomy. The Catholic Church might have accepted his views and incorporated them into its own rich variety of theological viewpoints. After all, the medieval church was by no means theologically monolithic, but always exhibited a wide diversity of opinion. Martin Luther might well have remained a faithful son of the Roman Church and died a respected Catholic theologian.

The question confronting the Catholic Church during the early years of controversy was thus whether Luther's theological emphasis might be incorporated under the broad mantle of true catholicity. As matters turned out, the answer given was negative, though one might suggest that this was not at all inevitable or necessary. To say this is not to deny the existence of some real theological divergences between Luther and the mainstream medieval tradition. But these differences were such as could be forgotten or ignored with silence. Early in 1519 Luther had assured the papal chamberlain Karl von Miltitz that he would not write anything further. This should have been a splendid opportunity to resolve a conflict in which the psychological setting and the temper of the several participants were more important than the actual disagreement over theological points. But both sides, Luther and those who took up his cause no less than his Catholic antagonists, failed to see this with sufficient clarity. If the Catholic Church showed itself unwilling to accept Luther as a legitimate option, then Luther can be said to have made it impossible for it to do otherwise. He was a person of explosive temper and he always wore his heart on his sleeve. Temperamentally, he was a bit cocky and exuberantly self-confident, persuaded as he was that he had opened the "gates of paradise" with his new understanding of Christianity. But Luther at times also had profound misgivings about the rightness of his views, and the question put to him by his Catholic opponents, "Are you the only one who is wise?" did not fail to haunt him.

The final decision in the matter was made in Rome—and that decision counted. It surely is not unfair to say that it was a hasty and hardly reflected decision, made under duress of time and on the urging of men like Eck. In any case, the bull *Exsurge Domine* was not a model summary of Luther's teaching. There were outright contradictions in the bull and some of the condemned propositions had not been taught by Luther in exactly the form stated. The bull gave little evidence that it had been drawn up after careful reflection. This characteristic of the document is important for understanding subsequent developments. On the face of things the official pronouncement should have settled the matter. Luther's tracts had been assessed and certain of his propositions were declared to be heretical. As far as the Catholic Church was concerned, the issue was closed.

The course of events was to show, however, that this final word was anything but final and that quite a few people were disposed to consider the bull merely a scrap of paper. A number of people, by no means partisans of Luther's cause, felt that he had not been treated fairly. This conviction threw sufficient sand into the legal machinery to reduce the papal bull to insignificance. A large chorus of voices favored giving Luther another hearing, since the one he had received had been superficial and had not taken him seriously. This sentiment led to Luther's appearance before the German diet at Worms in April 1521—a strange happening, indeed, for the condemnation by the Catholic Church should have settled the matter. Thus uncertainty characterized the situation both before and after the bull, and this did its share to keep Luther's proclamation from being squelched and Luther himself from suffering the fate of many heretics before him. Luther's appearance before the diet failed to accomplish anything—except that he picked up a few more followers who kept the issue alive. Afterward, the diet dutifully, but amidst legal confusion, issued an edict that declared Luther an outlaw.

But even this official pronouncement on the part of the German Empire did not settle the case of the heretic Martin Luther. Instead of suffering a violent death at the stake Luther was able to live out his life and die peacefully in bed. If we ask the reason for this surely unexpected turn of events, several answers suggest themselves. One was provided by none other than Emperor Charles himself when he remarked after his abdication that it had been the greatest mistake of his rule to have honored Luther's safe-conduct after Worms. There is a measure of truth in this reflection, for we can hardly overlook the powerful role played by the Wittenberg professor in subsequent events. But alone it does not suffice as explanation, for Luther actually was removed from the scene for almost a year following his dramatic appearance before the German diet at Worms and not a few people actually thought him dead. A far more incisive factor was the widespread and increasingly intense popular support for Luther. Here was not merely a "drunken German monk," as Pope Leo X had naively quipped, who had prompted the controversy, but a host of men who in a variety of ways made Luther's cause their own. They took to their pens and committed their thoughts to print. During the first years of the controversy Luther had borne the brunt of the literary battle; but as time went on he acquired numerous assistants. Not all of them were capable and most of them lacked creativity, but they all possessed a burning desire to further the cause of Luther—as they understood it.

Thus, Luther's word became print and indeed more than that: it became flesh, for from pulpits everywhere the Lutheran message resounded. Its spread was thereby vastly intensified. Catholic priests turned into staunch partisans of Luther. People throughout the land, listening to their preachers, no longer heard the proclamation of the old faith, such as they had known from the days of their youth, but a new evangel, new slogans, new doctrines, new principles. While the enormous circulation of Luther's tracts was an important means in spreading his message beyond Wittenberg, the contribution of countless ministers to the propagation of the new faith in the length and breadth of Germany was equally significant.

Within a few years Luther had found an army of devoted followers. The popular appeal of Luther's proclamation must not be overstated. That there was a response, at first vague and haphazard, then widespread and determined, is beyond doubt. But we must not assume that every man, woman, and child flocked to this new proclamation. Not everyone could read and acquaint himself with Luther's writings. And not all those who were able to read were interested in religious matters. In other words, we are speaking only of a limited segment of the populace—the intellectuals, the educated, the middle class—if an all-too-modern term is permissible—which must not be equated with society at large. Among these people support for Luther was extensive.

In part this support was due to a real commitment to Luther's religion, in part to an inadequate understanding of what he stood for. The fact is that Luther wore a coat of many colors: he could be seen as a German nationalist who asserted himself against Rome, as a humanist who echoed the concern for ecclesiastical change, as a social reformer who identified himself with the discontent with the existing state of society. The vagueness of Luther's early proclamation and the swiftness of the course of events made such divergent interpretations both possible and likely. If the papal nuncio Aleander reported from Germany in 1521 that nine-tenths of the people shouted "Luther," then one must not only question the numerical accuracy of his statement but also, and more significantly so, whether the people who so shouted knew what they were actually saying.

In short, Luther's cause had many strange bedfellows in those early years and the parting of the ways between Luther and some of his disciples which occurred later on was inevitable. But even afterward Luther's cause continued virtually unabated, an indication that it possessed real support. And this point must not be lost in overly sophisticated interpretations, for without the recognition that Luther's message somehow or other touched the religious feelings of his contemporaries we fail to comprehend his impact.

Luther confronted his contemporaries with a new interpretation of the Christian gospel, which, no matter how vaguely presented at first, proved sweetly attractive. Luther personalized religion, insisting that man's true service of God does not consist in the carrying out of externals, but in the free and spontaneous expression of faith. One might almost say that Luther simplified religion by advocating a religion based only on Scripture, only on faith with rules, regulations, theoretical distinctions dismissed as irrelevant. The Christian was called upon to put his trust in God. Religion was no longer complicated, no longer an oppressive external routine; it was faith.

At the same time, Luther made religion democratic. This is to say that he insisted that each individual personally apprehend and reflect upon the gospel. Luther's proclamation was the declaration of religious independence of the laity—of all those, in other words, who theretofore had stood on the sidelines and passively watched the religious pageant. When Luther placed a German version of the New Testament into the hands of the people in 1522, he carried out in actual practice what he had already theoretically espoused. The willingness and ability of laymen, untrained in theology, to discuss religious matters with more learned opponents was a characteristic of the early Reformation. Hans von der Planitz, a Saxon councillor at the Nuremberg *Reichsregiment,* for example, ably defended Luther and on one occasion retorted to the charge that monks were leaving the monasteries because of Luther's teaching that there was nothing wrong with their leaving, for the early church had not known monks.

To the popular dimension of Luther's cause must be added another one. The Edict of Worms had transformed Luther's cause into a legal case. As a result of this, legal maneuverings increasingly came to the fore after 1521. The prime question was whether the Edict could be administered in the German territories in the face of the intense support for Luther. Or, if it could not, what kind of *modus vivendi* could be found for the adherents of Luther's message? Accordingly, the focus of the ongoing course of events was legal and governmental. In the three years after Worms, the *Reichsregiment*, the "imperial regiment" that took the Emperor's place in his absence from Germany, had to address itself to the problem, not so much in order to formulate policy, but to see to the execution of the Edict during the Emperor's absence. The efforts remained unsuccessful and afterward a long succession of German diets from Speyer in 1526 to Augsburg in 1555 grappled with the religious problem. Each of these diets faced it in a different form, though basically the question always remained the same: Should the Edict of Worms be administered or rescinded? Should the Lutheran proclamation be accepted?

Thus the character of events changed after the Diet of Worms of May 1521. What had been a theological controversy over the opinions of one individual turned into the Reformation. Nothing illustrates this better than the fact that Martin Luther, who had precipitated the tumultuous happenings, increasingly faded from the limelight and ceased being the central figure. Naturally, his spirit was still very much present, as was the awareness that it had been his theological thought that had brought about this searching, if turbulent, reformulation of the Christian gospel. But from then on the story of the ecclesiastical transformation may well be told without Luther, who was content to pursue his round of academic activities at Wittenberg.

The years after Worms were a time of storm and stress during which Luther experienced the resounding popular response and the exuberant group of disciples that made for a movement of vast dimensions. At the same time, those years were a period of clarification during which men sought to delineate more carefully the implications of Luther's message. Up to this point its statements and concerns had been broad, comprehensive, and general. Then came the second thoughts, the critical scrutiny, the searching reassessment. And not all saw eye to eye, and naturally the ways parted.

It began in the fall of 1521 in Wittenberg. Luther was still in the castle of the Wartburg, but at Wittenberg some of his impatient peers demanded that whatever practical changes were demanded by the new understanding of the gospel should be undertaken at once: if the Mass was unscriptural, its celebration should be stopped immediately. Since others inclined toward a more cautious procedure, tensions arose in the city and in the end only Luther seemed to be able to save the day.

When he returned he took a stand against those who had advocated sweeping and immediate changes, arguing that externals should only be altered after the minds and hearts of the people had been changed. To effect ecclesiastical renewal by external fiat and by the introduction of new regulations was but another perversion of the gospel, no different from the existing practice. Moreover, Luther argued, the Christian faith knows not only rules but also freedom, and concerning some of its aspects no rigid rules exist. Luther advocated a reform at once conservative and modest. In the end it was this orientation that characterized the manner of ecclesiastical change in those places where his word counted.

A second parting of the ways came with the German peasant uprising of 1524/25. While the underlying causes for this uprising reach back into the fifteenth century and indicate, most of all, the uncertain place of the peasants in society, the grievances expressed by the peasants in 1524 had a new ring to them. They were clad in language taken straight from Luther's book—phrases like "the grace of God," the "word of God," "God's righteousness," which served as a kind of Lutheran embellishment to long-standing peasant concerns and demands. The peasants' most famous document, the *Twelve Articles* of 1525, demanded, for example, that ministers should preach only "the pure word of God" and be appointed by the congregation. They stated, moreover, that if any demand was found to be contrary to the Scriptures it would be disavowed. Luther had clearly made an impact on the peasants. As events were to show, however, the peasants were in for a profound disappointment.

The initially haphazard response of the authorities allowed the uprising to spread from its cradle in the southwest corner of Germany to South and Central Germany. At first the peasants' demands were moderate, and the possibility of concord existed. But it was not achieved. And this is the real tragedy of the uprising. As time passed, the peasants turned increasingly radical and the encounters with the forces of the rulers were marked by grim ruthlessness on both sides.

In the end, the peasants went down in defeat, for they were no match for the well armed soldiers of the rulers. As they went down, so did their hopes and aspirations, and so did Martin Luther whom many peasants saw as their mentor. Uncannily, the peasants' uprising had become part of the Reformation and a disastrous part at that. Luther had written two pamphlets dealing with the demands of the peasants, entitled *Friendly Admonition to Peace* and *Against the*

Murderous and Plundering Hordes of the Peasants. The latter clearly sided with the authorities and smote with harsh words the peasants, who were to be "slain, stabbed and killed" by the rulers. Afterward Luther was chided for having been double-tongued in the matter, at first having encouraged the peasants and then siding with the authorities. Actually, he had been consistent throughout, always rejecting the use of religion for the realization of social and economic goals. In the first of his two tracts he had in truth sympathized with the grievances of the peasants, but had insisted, nonetheless, that social and economic matters had to be settled by the experts in secular fields, rather than by experts in the gospel. But Luther was not only convinced that using the gospel in pursuit of social and economic goals was theologically wrong. He was also persuaded that it would have no beneficial result. The uprising would lead to anarchy—and anarchy would produce more injustice and harm than had tyranny. It was a deeply sensitive man who faced the turbulence of the peasants' uprising, sensitive to what he saw as the mandate of the gospel and sensitive to considerations of prudence. This is, surely, the deep irony of his confrontation with those who sought alleviation for some of the most pressing social problems of the time.

Chapter 4

The Political Consolidation in Germany

Five years after the Edict of Worms no one could doubt that this document was a scrap of paper. It had proved ineffective. Luther, and the movement that he had precipitated, were still very much alive. Lutheran pamphlets continued to issue from the printing presses and Lutheran preachers continued to propound the new faith. Indeed, at more and more places this evangelical proclamation led to new forms of ecclesiastical life: different forms of the divine service were used and new structures of organizational life were developed. No longer did a single professor of theology alone proclaim a new version of the Christian gospel; a movement had emerged and assumed ecclesiastical form.

Naturally, such could not be done without the support of governmental authority. No matter how extensive the popular enthusiasm for Luther's evangel, if the territorial rulers had remained hostile, no empirical consolidation could have taken place. Such was the case for two reasons: firstly, the rulers considered themselves responsible, in one way or another, also for ecclesiastical affairs and, secondly, they were the ones called upon to administer the Edict of Worms. The second reason was crucial, since the unwillingness on the part of some rulers to administer the Edict allowed the new faith to expand. A telling expression of this state of affairs came at the diet held in Speyer in 1526, when the time for a resolute suppression of Lutheranism had seemingly arrived. The unanimous stand of the territorial rulers against the rebelling peasants suggested that at long last they might be willing also to put down the Lutheran heresy since rebellion and heresy seemed but two sides of the same coin. But it turned out that Lutheran sentiment was astoundingly strong and after lengthy deliberations the estates could not agree on anything but that each ruler should deal with the Edict of Worms—that is, administer it or not administer it— in the way he felt he could justify standing before God and the Emperor. This provision was meant as a truce, a temporary solution, for the return of the Emperor to Germany was presently expected and hope prevailed that he would bring the contested religious issue to an acceptable conclusion.

This temporary provision of 1526 determined the development that was to characterize subsequent German history: each ruler decided the religion in his realm. To be sure, another thirty years were to pass in Germany before this temporary provision was made definitive and the 1555 Peace of Augsburg legalized the rulers' right to reform. The path, however, was cleared in 1526.

Naturally, the question arises why some rulers were willing to embrace the new faith. Man being what he is, one suspects that concrete political advantages must have accrued from so doing. No doubt, there is some truth in this and illustrations for ecclesiastical maneuvering for political advantages are not hard to find. The appetite may here well have come with the eating. As we have had occasion to note, the place of the political authorities in ecclesiastical affairs had steadily increased during the fifteenth century and in the main the authorities possessed such power over ecclesiastical matters as they desired. But the religious controversy precipitated by Luther may have suggested to some that an opportune hour had come to usurp such ecclesiastical independence and prerogatives as still remained. At stake was not so much the ruler's intrusion in the inner affairs of the church, the way it believed and worshiped, but the numerous rights and prerogatives, both legal and financial, enjoyed by the church, which made it virtually a state within the state. This was the thorn in the flesh of the rulers, and the religious upheaval may have suggested a painless solution.

Some rulers, however, exhibited a genuine religious commitment. There were men who had been touched by the new evangel and their public policies were but the outward expression of their inner conviction. To uphold this conviction in the early years of reformatory change required a good deal of conviction. In later years the adherents of the Protestant faith enjoyed a measure of political and military stature which assured them safety; in the 1520s, however, the support of an outlaw and heretic was a touchy matter. When the Margrave of Brandenburg told Emperor Charles at Augsburg in 1530 that he would rather have his head cut off than attend Mass, he expressed his commitment to a religious cause. And even Landgrave Philipp of Hesse, youthful, impulsive, sensuous, politically concerned, gave evidence in those years of an authentic religious orientation.

The centrality of the territorial rulers meant the program of theological renewal advocated by Martin Luther became an affair of state, presented by governmental officials at official gatherings, by lawyers and councillors, by legal arguments and considerations. To be sure, while the lawyers and councillors did so at the gatherings of the German estates, someone stayed at home and kept the fires burning—ministers preached from their pulpits and counseled their flocks; theologians expounded the faith—and perhaps that was what counted. The formal decisions, however, were made elsewhere.

This political involvement of the Reformation led inextricably to political alliances and, in the end, to war. As early as 1524 several Catholic rulers agreed to form an alliance against the "damned Lutheran sect" and within a short time several Lutheran rulers had formed an opposing alliance. In 1528 came an illustration par excellence of the precarious state of tempers, when the maneuverings of one Otto von Pack brought the two camps to the brink of war. Pack had revealed to Landgrave Philipp of Hesse the existence of a Catholic plan to wage war on the Lutherans and Philipp promptly prepared for a defensive war in turn. As it turned out, the plan had been in Pack's head only, but Philipp's credulence indicated that a danger obviously existed.

The quest for a formal alliance of the adherents of the new faith reached its successful conclusion in 1531 with the founding of the League of Schmalkald, comprised of those Protestant territories and cities willing to accept the Augsburg Confession, the statement of faith submitted by the Lutherans at the Diet of Augsburg in 1530. No matter what its weaknesses, and there were several, this League proved an important factor in German politics for almost two decades. It was the political embodiment of Protestantism in Germany and its existence left little doubt but that any attempt to solve the religious question would have to reckon with this alliance.

The 1530s and 1540s brought one attempt after the other to resolve the religious problem. Whenever a diet met, it addressed itself to the issue, but each time with inconclusive results. This state of affairs allowed the Protestant faith to expand and to consolidate, for as long as the religious problem remained unsolved the Protestants were able to breathe freely and faced no difficulties.

The failure to solve the problem had several reasons. In the first place, a great deal of vagueness prevailed concerning the real issues that kept the two sides apart. Were they certain ecclesiastical practices, such as the withholding of the communion cup from the laity or the celibacy of the clergy? Or was the divergence theological in nature, such as a different understanding of the sacraments or of the church? Today these questions can be easily answered; then, uncertainty and even confusion prevailed which made for haphazard and difficult situations.

A second point is closely related. Men on both sides, such as Melanchthon and Bucer among the Protestants, Gropper and Contarini among the Catholics, found the unity of Christendom an important consideration and declared themselves unwilling to face a schism. Their ecumenical sentiment propelled the efforts at conciliation forward from one attempt to the next and this delayed the eventual showdown. But both sides also had their more rigid and less conciliatory protagonists, men such as Eck and Luther, and these were more influential.

Last, but not least, there was a political consideration. Only one man might have been able to secure uniform ecclesiastical practice in Germany—the Emperor, who by virtue of both his temperament and his office thought it his responsibility to look beyond the confines of the individual territories and be concerned about the Empire at large. Charles V was prepared to exercise this function. Indeed, from his youth he had dreamed of his role as the guardian of Christendom, had aspired to recreate the empire of Charlemagne and rule over a domain on which the sun would never set, where all men would live in peace and harmony in the true Catholic faith.

But between the desire and the act, between the thought and deed, fell the shadow. No matter how noble and high his aspirations, Charles could not carry them out. Once he had observed that he wanted to be known to posterity as the emperor during whose rule the Lutheran heresy had made its appearance and had been crushed. But this remained only an aspiration, for his religious policy failed miserably. It did so largely because he always had too many irons in the fire, some of which necessitated long absences from Germany. Immediately after the Diet of Worms in 1521 he had left Germany, not to return until nine years later. He stayed for about a year—only to be gone again for almost another decade. His Spanish domains, his chronic conflict with France, together with the Turkish menace constituted problems that required attention.

The external course of events in Germany was such that the diet at Speyer in 1529 rescinded the recess of 1526. Thereby the administration of the Edict of Worms was once again made mandatory. The supporters of the new faith, while only a minority, vigorously objected to this decision. Their protest gave them the label of Protestants, which came to be their standard appellation throughout Europe. In addition to a name—it actually was a mistranslation of the Latin *protestari sumus* ("we testify")—their protest also granted them a breather, for their resoluteness suggested a new approach to the solution of the religious problem. Since the Emperor's return was imminent, the possibility of a resolution of the problem with his help seemed real.

The diet gathering at Augsburg during the summer of 1530 was convened for this purpose. It was accordingly preoccupied with the religious issue and Charles made a determined effort at reconciliation. Though a Catholic at heart, he hoped that by making modest concessions a way out of the dilemma might be found. He was mistaken both about the nature of the conflict and the temperament of the protagonists, for the gap between the two sides was wider than he seemed to realize. Moreover, he had to discover that intimately related to the religious turmoil was the eminent political problem of the day: something had to be done about the Turks who stood outside Vienna and threatened to storm westward. To counter them, Charles needed troops and thus money, which had to come from the territorial rulers. The pursestrings were held in part by Protestant rulers who were naturally indisposed to render financial support to an Emperor who seemed, in the same breath, to ask them for money and to threaten to subdue them by force. The situation was complex indeed and in the end the diet agreed on a compromise. The Protestants were told to return to the Catholic fold or the Emperor would take appropriate action against them, but they received a period of grace until April of the following year.

The situation at Augsburg proved paradigmatic for the years to come: the importance of the religious question on the agenda of the diet, the uncertainty as to the real nature of the religious conflict, the impingement of political and financial considerations, the Emperor's helplessness, the inconclusiveness of the negotiations. The specific emphases may have differed with different diets; the basic ingredients, however, remained the same. Still, the efforts persisted, from year to year, from diet to diet—Regensburg in 1532 and 1541, Speyer in 1542 and 1544, Regensburg in 1546. A major milestone came in 1540/41 when Charles succeeded in getting the two sides together for theological colloquies at Worms and Regensburg. Surprisingly enough, both instances brought some agreements. Indeed, at Regensburg both sides agreed on the doctrine of justification. It was a rather simple and vague statement that both sides accepted, but still it was an agreement on that crucial point of controversy around which seemed to revolve all other theological differences. But this agreement proved to be a drop in the bucket, for in the end theological discord prevailed even at Regensburg—and this convinced the Emperor that irenic conciliation was out of the question. At long last, he faced the situation realistically and decided to resolve the religious problem by going to war. Since he had waited almost three decades before doing so, one can grant that he had exhausted every other possibility before deciding to take that fateful step.

He waited for the opportune time, which came in the fall of 1546. Charles' pretense for the war was political and this allowed him to keep some parties neutral and even pick up some Protestant allies, such as Moritz of Saxony. In the War of Schmalkald, as the conflict is known, even the Schmalkaldians, who had for some years exhibited the bickering and uncertainty that seem to befall all alliances after an initial danger has passed, had a chance for the laurels of victory. But confusion, ineptness, and timidity brought about their eventual downfall, dramatically exemplified by the defeat of the Saxon forces by the Emperor at Mühlberg in March 1547.

Afterward Charles V sought to put his house in order and in so doing he once again proved to be his own worst enemy by pursuing plans that were hopelessly unrealistic and bound to fail. Not only did he seek to crush Protestantism—and even this was easier said than done, however, since some of his own allies were Protestants—but he also sought to strengthen imperial power in the Empire. He must have thought himself strong enough to do both at the same time; events were to show that he was bitterly mistaken. Some of his allies, notably the new Saxon Elector Moritz, deserted him and his position was weakened. Before long he faced a formidable constellation of political opposition in Germany through a conspiracy of territorial rulers. His proposal for a solution of the religious problem, promulgated at the diet of Augsburg in 1547/8, had not endeared him to many people either. It had basically decreed the re-establishment of Catholicism, with a few temporary concessions granted to the Protestants. The temporary character of the concessions led to the label INTERIM. Naturally, the Protestants objected, but so did the Catholics, who argued that the Emperor had no business meddling in religious and ecclesiastical affairs by offering concessions, even temporary ones, to the Protestants.

In the face of these difficulties which wrested the fruit of his military victory from him Charles once again temporized, used big words about his plans and for the time being postponed the inevitable showdown. But the years before the War of Schmalkald had shown theological conciliation to be impossible and the aftermath of the war itself had proved the use of force a failure. Nothing was left but to recognize the Protestants once and for all. But Charles would have nothing to do with this. He left Germany and his brother Ferdinand had to preside over the bankruptcy of his religous policy at the Diet of Augsburg in 1555. The Peace of Augsburg, agreed upon after many months of negotiations, brought the legal recognition of Lutheranism in Germany by giving the territorial rulers the right to determine the ecclesiastical orientation of their territories. Their subjects had to accept his decision—or emigrate to a more desirable ecclesiastical climate. There were other complicated provisions in the Peace—for example, the Protestantization of ecclesiastical territories up to 1552 was recognized while changes after that date were to be personal changes on the part of the ruler only—but this one, subsequently embodied in the phrase *cuius regio, eius religio,* overshadowed them all.

Almost thirty-five years had passed since the day the youthful Charles V had first gone on record with his determination to crush the Lutheran menace. He had worked hard and long to live up to his pledge but Augsburg showed that he had failed. Irony hovers over

Charles's place in the history of the Reformation in the sixteenth century, for more so than most actors on the stage of events, he sensed the gravity of the drama being played and the seriousness of a divided Christendom. He pursued his policies doggedly and with a measure of commitment that should have earned him a larger support from the ranks of the Catholics than was the case. But since his devotion to the Catholic cause was mixed with his own particular appraisal of the situation, his mission was doomed to failure almost from the beginning. Men who fail are hardly ever attractive figures in the narratives of history. Charles V is here no exception.

Chapter 5

The European Dimension

If it was Luther's most noteworthy characteristic that he was not executed as a heretic but lived to see the establishment of Lutheran churches, then the fact that his proclamation resulted in a movement of European dimension surely was an accomplishment of equal significance. Luther's brand of ecclesiastical transformation and his interpretation of Christian faith did not remain confined to Germany, but spread throughout Europe. Only Ireland, Spain, and Italy remained untouched by Protestantism, and even in the latter two countries Protestant sentiment made a bold, though abortive, appearance.

This European dimension of the Reformation can be seen either as the direct result of Luther's proclamation or as the autonomous emergence of religious concerns akin to those of Luther. Both have been argued. French historians, for example, have insisted that the origins of the French Reformation should not be sought with Luther but with Jacques Lefèvre and other like-minded French humanists, while English scholars have pointed to the survival of Lollardy in early sixteenth-century England and the theological independence of the early English reformers.

The evidence on the other side of the fence, however, seems persuasive. Luther's early tracts were widely circulated throughout Europe and about the spread of his ideas there can be little doubt. In specific instances such as Tyndale in England, Petri in Sweden, or Tausen in Denmark, one can cite chapter and verse where the native reformers took their material straight from him. Of course, only the basic and elementary of Luther's thoughts lent themselves to easy propagation abroad, those notions with catchy slogans and simple labels, such as "justification by faith," "by Scripture alone," etc. But Luther's tracts were read by men who possessed a theological understanding and competence of their own, whose prior involvement in the pursuit of the Christian gospel disposed them to react favorably to the new word coming from Germany. By no means were they theological *tabulae rasae;* they enriched their own theological background and understanding with those facets of Luther's writings that seemed attractive. Luther influenced but he never overpowered; he stimulated, but never dominated. The native reformers always occupied the central place, but they are unthinkable without Luther.

The problem of language kept Luther's tracts from making the same direct popular appeal as had been the case in Germany, where he had extensively used the vernacular—as illustrated by his *Open Letter to the Christian Nobility*—and where even his Latin pamphlets were promptly translated into German. Elsewhere in Europe, the vernacular Protestant tracts were written by the native reformers, who retained their own particular theological orientation even though they plagiarized extensively from Luther.

Several features characterized this European expansion, particularly the time lag between the theological controversy in Germany and that elsewhere in Europe. Not until the late 1520s did the Lutheran message find protagonists throughout Europe. By that time much of the ecclesiastical transformation in Germany had already been accomplished, even though in certain countries such as Sweden, the change was completed long before that in Germany, a tell-tale sign that the process elsewhere in Europe could be smoother and speedier as well.

The European pattern of ecclesiastical transformation conformed to that in Germany. There was agitation for ecclesiastical reform and theological innovation, a popular response, a mixture of concerns, both religious and non-religious. And in Europe no less than in Germany the Reformation was an affair of state. That is to say, in the final analysis the question of ecclesiastical change lay in the hands of those who exercised political authority and power. More than that, the manner of ecclesiastical change in the various countries conformed to the religious propensity exhibited by those who were in control. England and King Henry VIII is a splendid case in point.

The initial Lutheran impact upon Europe was subsequently replaced by the Calvinist form of Protestantism which scored the most striking successes in France, Hungary, Poland, Scotland, and Holland. Naturally, this fact raises certain questions: Was Calvinism the more persuasive form of Protestantism? Was it more congenial to the European mind than the Teutonically oriented gospel according to Luther? A satisfactory answer comes only with difficulty, though one might say that wherever Protestantism achieved speedy success—foremostly in Scandinavia, of course—it was Lutheran in propensity. On the other hand, wherever the struggle for formal recognition was not concluded by the 1540s Calvinism won out. And this for the simple reason that by that time Lutheranism was a house bitterly divided, beset by theological conflicts, fighting a life-or-death struggle for its survival in the face of the Emperor's attempt to re-introduce Catholicism in Germany after the War of Schmalkald. Calvinism, on the other hand, was able to boast of the most eminent theologian of the second generation of the Reformation, namely Calvin, and was unperturbed by the kind of inner strife that rendered Lutheranism weak and impotent.

A full account of the European dimension of the Protestant Reformation is impossible here for lack of space and the reader is spared, therefore, a lengthy exposition. We wish to avoid a confusing narration of a bewildering multiplicity of events or complexity of developments. Four countries, England, France, Sweden, and Poland (one might say that they represent the four points of the compass) have been selected for brief accounts that reveal interesting and different patterns of ecclesiastical transformation.

It will quickly become apparent that the course of events in each of these countries underlines what has already been observed in a general fashion: that the place of the political ruler in the quest for ecclesiastical change was a central one and that in the final analysis, therefore, the reformatory proclamation had to relate itself to the political realities of the concrete situation. Only if this was done successfully could the new faith be victorious. This chapter will show how the political situation differed in each instance and how the proclamation of the new faith had to accommodate and adapt itself to this. In England a conservative, indeed Catholic, monarch separated from the Roman church for other than theological or ecclesiastical reasons. In Sweden another strong monarch determined the political scene. Since the ruler was not so determinedly Catholic as in England, however, the Swedish development showed a more distinct Protestant propensity. France and Poland, finally, lacked a strong ruler. Considerable power was exercised by the nobility in France, some of whom, unlike the nobility in Poland, attached themselves to the Protestant cause for political as well as religious reasons. This meant that in France Protestantism was politically strong enough to counter all Catholic moves at suppression and the final showdown concerning the new faith was postponed until the end of the century.

To study the Reformation sixteenth-century Europe can mean different things to different people—the spread of Protestant ideas, the emergence of different forms of Protestant church life, the extent of eventual Protestant success. Our remarks are only concerned with the last of these aspects and will attempt to show the influence of extraneous factors on the course of events.

England

England can boast a record when it comes to reformatory upheaval. Four times between 1530 and 1560 the official religion in the land was changed—and each time the change occurred at the behest of the ruler. Henry VIII first cut the ecclesiastical ties with Rome and transformed English religion into an intriguing kind of non-Roman Catholicism. His son Edward VI—or rather his son's advisers—introduced a pronounced form of Protestantism, while his daughter Mary took the country officially back to the state of ecclesiastical affairs such as had prevailed before Henry had begun to meddle in them. The brevity of Mary's reign allowed her half-sister Elizabeth to bring about a religious settlement of a moderately Protestant character. And this settlement survived the eroding sands of time despite vehement attacks from both left and right, from ardent Protestants no less than determined Catholics. Four changes in thirty years! Englishmen, born soon after the turn of the century and attaining the patriarchal age of four-score years, had to adjust their ecclesiastical routine, if not their faith, five times during their lives—surely a strange commentary on the intensity of ecclesiastical change of sixteenth-century Europe.

The changes undertaken by Henry VIII stand at the beginning and set the pattern for what was to follow. They were oriented by both the

King's temper and his particular predicament. Accordingly, no narrative of the English Reformation can avoid affording the central place to that all too self-confident, astute, and arrogant monarch whose hand lay heavily on the ecclesiastical events. What precipitated the ecclesiastical change in England was "the King's great matter," as the euphemistic label had it, or "the divorce," a more obvious but equally misleading description of Henry's desire to have his marriage to Catherine of Aragon declared invalid on the ground that it was prohibited by divine law since it violated an impediment of affinity (Catherine was his elder brother Arthur's widow). Whether Henry really was perturbed about having broken the law of God, as he himself so movingly insisted, will forever remain a mystery. He seems mainly to have been concerned about a male heir—even though Catherine was perennially pregnant she had failed to produce a son —and also interested in a new candidate for the royal bed. In both respects he eventually had his way; to reach his goals, however, he had to break with the Roman Church.

The King's desire for an annulment of his marriage by the pope did not find receptive ears in the papacy. The political situation of the late 1520s had brought Pope Clement VII under the domination of Emperor Charles who, as Catherine's uncle, had every reason to obstruct Henry's desire. Henry waited patiently for almost half a decade until he realized that as matters stood he could not expect positive word from Rome. He tried ecclesiastical blackmail by having Parliament pass the Conditional Restraint of Annates, which threatened to withhold the annates, the first year's income from ecclesiastical positions, from the curia. He tried to rally learned opinion against the pope by canvassing the universities of Christendom for their verdict concerning the biblical legitimacy of his marriage. Theoretically, this had been a skillful move, first put forth by an unknown Cambridge don who was to play a major role in the subsequent Reformation in England, Thomas Cranmer. Practically, however, it proved to be an abject failure, for the academicians showed themselves hopelessly divided in their sentiment and, as often as not, the desires of various political authorities determined the academicians' opinions.

Matters remained at a standstill, until Henry's adviser Thomas Cromwell suggested that he was the sovereign of an empire, of an independent realm, in other words, which allowed him to resolve all issues within it on his own terms. And so it happened. A number of ecclesiastical changes were effected by several parliamentary statutes. The most relevant one, as far as the King was concerned, was that which declared him "supreme head of the church." The substance of these changes lay not so much in the realm of theology as in the severing of the ties of the English church with Rome.

This was the way the King wanted it. Since his own theological temperament was conservative, he saw no reason to engage in fancy theological reformulations. For a while he tolerated the dissemination of Protestant propaganda—after all, he could do with as much support against the pope as possible—and even sponsored an English Bible. Then he had second thoughts, and during the last ten years of his rule formally affirmed Catholic tenets.

Henry VIII, his quest for a divorce, his theological propensity, were thus the prime factors in the ecclesiastical transformation in England. The King's *placet* made its legal expression possible. But this fact should not mislead us to assume that such was the whole story of ecclesiastical change. It was not. Henry's legal maneuvers took place against the backdrop not only of the reformatory upheaval on the Continent but also the agitation for ecclesiastical and theological change in England itself. England had its share of proponents of such change, men who had imbibed the new theology coming forth from the Continent and who were persuaded that religious change could also be effected in England. At Cambridge men like Robert Barnes and William Tyndale met in the White Horse Inn which was promptly dubbed "little Germany." They agitated for ecclesiastical reform and thus introduced extensive theological discussion to the English scene. How widespread this sentiment was is another question, though there is little doubt but that those interested in religion were conscious of the ongoing theological turmoil.

Thus, a religious factor is present after all. What Henry VIII sought to undertake in England is unthinkable without the religious atmosphere in the country. It is also unthinkable without the continental precedent suggesting itself for imitation in England. The King together with his brilliant advisor Cromwell must surely have been aware of it even if they never said so. The Protestant rulers on the Continent had shown that the cutting of ties with Rome and the replacement of papal authority by the ruler could be done rather successfully.

Once the ties with Rome had been cut, the religious scene in England became even livelier and Protestant agitation was even more pronounced. The King's anti-Roman orientation made for a relatively tolerant situation in England, where tracts and pamphlets with a Protestant orientation issued with increasing frequency from the printing presses.

The ecclesiastical change in England poses the question of the influence of Christian humanism and Erasmus on the Reformation. While it is, in varying ways, important for other European countries also, it is particularly pertinent for England, where the kind of religious reform concretely undertaken seems to echo the ideals of Christian humanism. Henry VIII ordered Erasmus' *Paraphrases* on the Gospels to be placed in all churches. The stress on moderate theological and ecclesiastical reform together with an emphasis on the ethical component of the Christian religion, such as characterized the English Reformation, was well-nigh identical with the program of ecclesiastical renewal propounded by Erasmus. The suggestion, therefore, that the English humanists exerted considerable influence upon the religious transformation in their country appears well founded.

Erasmus cannot be easily dismissed as a godfather of the English Reformation. He had spent some time in England and while he never came to appreciate the land (nor its beer!), his influence was far-reaching. In the 1530s, when the shape of the ecclesiastical transformation was hammered out in England, a remarkable number of his writings were translated into English and his *Paraphrases* of the New Testament was officially sponsored at the same time. Both are indications of the relevance he was evidently thought to have for the issues of ecclesiastical change and reorientation.

If there is thus little doubt about Erasmus' impact on the English scene, we must not overstate the case. Virtually all the reformers (with the notable exception of Luther himself) had been humanists of the Erasmian variety before they became reformers. What is argued for England would need to hold true for the Continent as well—only it does not. In England other influences were also at work, the Continental reformers and the Lollard tradition, for example, and together they determined the course of events. The great premises in England were the King's theological temper and the assertion of the royal supremacy. This would seem to offer as much of a clue to the Reformation in that land as the thought of the peripatetic humanist from Rotterdam.

The incisive ecclesiastical change in England during the rule of Henry VIII was the rejection of papal jurisdiction. It was not the only change, however. There were others: the most spectacular one the dissolution of the monasteries, which began in 1535 and lasted for the remainder of the decade. Once again a problem of the King stood in the center. This time it was financial, in part of his own making, in part the result of the general economic situation. Governmental finances were in desperate straits and short of levying new taxes (the most unpopular of all policies) no solution was in sight. But there was the property of the church, especially the monasteries, which were often wealthy. Their wealth promised to end the King's financial worries.

And so it happened. The official version was that the low quality of monastic life made the dissolution inevitable, but the real motivation was the property of the monasteries. England witnessed a financial transaction of major proportions. The King astutely disposed of the monastic property, did away with potential propaganda centers for the old church, ended his financial worries and, more than that, created a hard core of supporters of his religious policy, for those who benefited from the acquisition of the monastic lands could hardly advocate the re-establishment of the Catholic Church. All in all, the country lost an institution that in centuries past had not only provided lodging, food, and education to the people, but had symbolized religion itself.

The dissolutions precipitated a popular reaction, which showed that some Englishmen felt strongly enough about their old religion to rise up in arms on its behalf. The so-called Pilgrimage of Grace in 1536, a convenient label for several uprisings in Lincolnshire and Yorkshire, was a conservative rebellion. Those who voiced their grievances wanted the undoing of the recent ecclesiastical changes and innovations, in particular the dissolution of the monasteries. Their complaints were an odd mixture of religious and economic demands (in some instances they were only economic), such as were frequently voiced during the early sixteenth century. For a while the rebels seemed to have the upper hand against a fumbling king, but then Henry's ruthlessness brought about their collapse.

When Henry died in 1547, England was walking an ecclesiastical tightrope. The heart of the Catholic faith had been rejected and anti-Roman propaganda encouraged. No formal profession of Protestant ideals was possible. The country had learned to live with Protestant theory and Catholic practice. Aside from those who comforted themselves that their loyalty to the King came first or that the true Catholic faith was unimpaired, the good Catholics and the good Protestants in the land could not but hope for a change. It came with the succession of Edward VI, which brought the latent Protestant sentiment in high places out into the open. Since Edward was a child, power was exercised by a council of regency which was dominated first by Duke Somerset, and subsequently by John Dudley, Duke of Northumberland. Both steered the official ecclesiastical policy in England onto a distinctly Protestant course.

The most graphic expression came with the introduction of the *Book of Common Prayer* in 1549. For the English-speaking world, the Prayer Book is one of the most significant documents to come from the sixteenth century. The eminence of the Book lies both in its form and its content. The beauty of its prose rarely has been matched, but its chief accomplishment was the translation of the divine service into the vernacular. At long last, the people could understand as well as listen. What they heard was a moderate form of Protestantism, one that departed from the conservative theological atmosphere that had prevailed to the close of Henry's reign. A second edition of the Prayer Book came three years later and it was more pronouncedly Protestant. Indeed, if Communion may be taken as the measuring stick for theological orientation, the second Prayer Book took official religion in England so far to the left (that ominous direction) as it ever was to go. The Communion elements were taken as mere memorials of Christ's death; no real presence of Christ in the sacrament was acknowledged.

The formal ecclesiastical changes between 1547 and 1553 are clear enough, while the actual religious sentiment in the land is an "enigma wrapped in a mystery." Given a low level of theological literacy, one suspects that most folks were a bit bewildered by the changes that were going on. The well-known visitation record of Bishop Hooper, who in the early 1550s queried the clergy in his diocese about the fundamentals of the faith, the Ten Commandments, the Lord's Prayer, and the Apostles' Creed, reveals a shocking ignorance among the divines who were to be inspiration and example to their flocks. If most divines did not know who had taught the Lord's Prayer, the simple folk must have walked in even greater religious darkness.

It is worthy of note that in England religious conformity was not enforced with the same kind of ill-humored rigidity as was the case on the Continent. The parliamentary acts introducing the first and the second Prayer Book included some penalty provisions for non-adherence, but they were mild and pertained mainly to the use of another worship than that of the Prayer Book. In a sense, therefore, the provisions applied only to the clergy and left the people untouched. Such tolerance was unique in Europe.

After five years of Edwardian rule came the reign of Mary Tudor and her well-meant but ill-timed effort to reinstate Catholicism. She was the most pious of the Tudors (which does not say much), but received the ugliest appellation: Bloody Mary. Like her half-brother, Mary ruled for only half a decade and, if nothing else, the brevity of her rule spelled disaster for her effort. Actually, more than that must be said. England had not known the Catholic religion for almost a generation. During that time it had been illegal and attacked with unceasing polemical argumentation. Contrary to other European countries, there had been no running battle between the old and the new faith, no tug-of-war for the ear or the favor of the ruler. Catholicism had been out ever since 1532 and even though many people may have cared little one way or the other about official ecclesiastical labels, they simply did not have the background to rally enthusiastically to Mary's cause. Moreover, frequently the people who counted had some personal stake in the retention of the status quo, having had a share in the distribution of the monastic property. Thus, Parliament proved a hesitant partner in the Queen's efforts to restore Catholicism and this would seem weighty evidence for the true sentiment in the land.

But Mary had her way and Catholicism was made the formal religion of the English people. Those in positions of ecclesiastical eminence or with religious conviction had to abjure their Protestant "contamination," changing religion like one would change clothes, or make for the safety of the Protestant lands on the Continent. Some preferred the former course of action, some the latter. A few stood up for their conviction. They are the Marian martyrs of whom Archbishop Thomas Cranmer, burned at the stake in 1555, was the most famous. At the time, the Marian persecution did its modest share to make Catholic religion distasteful to Englishmen; conformity imposed by fire and sword hardly suggests an emotional attachment. Once the Queen had disappeared from the scene, the English people were ready for a change of ecclesiastical sentiment. And if their own experience was not sufficient to create a distaste for things Catholic, the eloquent pen of John Foxe did the rest. Foxe's *Acts and Monuments*, or *Book of Martyrs*, as it is commonly known, swathed an astoundingly accurate account of the Marian persecution with an emotionally Protestant embellishment. His account was eloquent as well as edifying and it turned into a major work of the English tongue, a piece of anti-Catholic propaganda that molded in its own way the religious temperament of the English people.

The ecclesiastical change occurring at the succession of Mary's half-sister Elizabeth in 1559 seemed almost inevitable. As daughter of Anne Boleyn, Elizabeth was a bastard in the eyes of the Catholic Church. This hardly disposed her to embrace that Church. Moreover, she may have sensed a religious weariness among Englishmen after the years of religious persecution. At any rate, she was a much better statesman than her half-sister and realized that Protestantism was more acceptable to the English people than Catholicism. But a break with Rome left all sorts of possibilities as to how far to go, and at first Elizabeth seemingly was content to return to the state of affairs which had existed in the closing years of her father's rule: an essentially conservative religion, distinguishable from its Roman counterpart mainly by the rejection of papal supremacy.

But the new Queen had to discover the strength of Protestant sentiment in Parliament. In an initial expression of that diplomatic prowess that was to make her a gifted ruler, she changed her mind and approved a religious settlement that reintroduced Protestantism of the sort that had prevailed under her half-brother Edward. And in a gesture that was as much a recognition of the misogyny of the age as of Elizabeth's own modest understanding of her position in the church, she designated her title as that of Supreme Governor (rather than Head) of the Church of England. Theologically the settlement of 1559 was vague, perhaps even conservative. In a way it came close to the ideal professed by some of the early reformers who sought to undertake a few ecclesiastical changes but in the main let the time-honored tradition of the church continue.

This conservative settlement occurred at a time when Calvinism was the exuberant form of Protestantism throughout Europe. It had been savored firsthand by many English Protestants who had preferred the safety of the Continent to the hazards of Marian England. When they returned to England upon Elizabeth's succession they were determined to realize some of its insights in their homeland—and promptly attacked the settlement. Perhaps such was the inevitable consequence of an arrangement that sought to travel the middle of the road between a pronounced Protestantism on the one hand and Catholicism on the other. The story of English ecclesiastical life during the remainder of the century depicts a persistent attack upon the settlement from Catholics who thought it too radical and from Protestants who thought it too mild and endowed with too much "popery." The English religious scene was lively, and England experienced the kind of religious turmoil and debate that had earlier characterized the Continent.

The staunch Protestants soon received a label of Puritans. Coined, like so many historical appellations, by opponents, it was to suggest that the Puritans were concerned about a pure and apostolic Christian faith. They wanted simplicity (which they took to be both a biblical norm and dictum) in worship as well as earnestness in life. No liturgical pageantry with ornate vestments, choreographic movements of the priest's hands and the worshippers' knees, or lighthearted demeanor on the Sabbath for them. But lest the label of Puritan evoke in our minds the image of sour-faced, drably clad men and women, dedicated to the proposition that anything joyful is sin, we must note that the sixteenth-century Puritan (in contrast to those who followed afterward) was above all concerned about religion, and not the minutiae of daily life. The Puritans desired further ecclesiastical reform in England, and they were persuaded that for this reform a biblical mandate existed. Their specific concerns varied at different stages of the way. At first, clerical vestments were at issue, with the Puritans contending that they were "Aaron's habits" and a papist abomination. Afterward the form of congregational polity became a matter of controversy, for the Puritans argued that the New Testament taught a presbyterian form of church government. There were other issues also, most of them in themselves trite and insignificant, but for the two sides symptoms of more fundamental differences. Did the Scriptures spell out the details of practical churchmanship, such as liturgy or clerical vestments? Here the two sides parted company, for the Puritans gave an emphatically affirmative answer, while their opponents thought this a matter of freedom.

Despite their vehement opposition to the Elizabethan settlement, the Puritans did not mean to separate from the Church of England. Somehow or other they thought it possible to bring about a revision along lines they considered both congenial and biblical. They were mistaken, for the ongoing controversy increasingly hardened tempers and stiffened positions and by the end of the century the earlier broadminded attitudes were a thing of the past. This was the irony of the eminent contribution of Richard Hooker, whose monumental *Laws of Ecclesiastical Polity,* begun in 1594, delineated the genius of Anglican flexibility and yet showed that the Puritan stance was outside that of the Anglican church. By that time, some of the Puritans realized that there was indeed no room for them in the Anglican inn and they consciously set out to chart their own ecclesiastical course.

Despite the perennial challenges of the Elizabethan settlement of religion, the settlement and with it English Protestantism survived virtually unscathed into the seventeenth century. Only then did a tumultuous development, in which (even as in the sixteenth century) religion and politics were inextricably woven together, lead to large-scale dissent from Anglican ranks. But the Church of England survived even that, aided by the political course of events after 1660. Part of this strength surely lay in the doctrinal latitude of the Church of England, foremostly expressed in the thirty-nine Articles of 1571.

France

The course of the Reformation in France might be cited as an instance where Protestantism was almost (but only almost) successful. The impact of Protestant ideas and the political strength of the Protestant movement were such as to take the country to the verge of accepting the Protestant faith. But in the end stood failure, perhaps inevitable from the very beginning, since French society was characterized by certain striking, if peculiar, features.

To begin with, the position of the French King in relation to the church was so powerful and influential that there was little, if any, political *raison d'être* for rejecting the Catholic Church. The French King was master in his mansion—and that included the church. What is more, no spectacular point of tension comparable to Henry VIII's "great matter" existed between the French crown and the papacy, and Francis I accordingly never found himself in that touchy situation where he had to make decisions against the church. Since the king was the authority in the land, he occupied the decisive place in the determination of its religious future. Only if he could be swayed by the Protestant message was there any possibility of effecting ecclesiastical change.

Reformation scholars continue to be divided about the origins of the French Reformation. Some see them in the reforming efforts of Bishop Briçonnet at Meaux; others point to the influx of Luther's ideas into the country. Perhaps the problem is one of nomenclature. If Reformation signifies the effort to reform the life of the church and attain a new theological understanding, then Briçonnet surely deserves priority. If, on the other hand, the term suggests a conscious break with the Catholic Church, then Luther's significance must be unquestioned, for the Catholic loyalty of Briçonnet or Lefèvre never waned.

The initial response of the authorities to Protestantism was routinely Catholic, though a bit haphazard, if for no other reason than the fact that in the 1520s the struggle with Spain—expressed by the battle of Pavia, the Peace of Madrid, the League of Cognac, the Peace of Cambrai—occupied the full attention of the country (and its king). Not until the placards affair of 1534, when Protestant handbills were posted one night at all sorts of places, including the door of the king's bedroom, did the Protestant proclamation imply a political danger and prompt Francis I at long last to act more resolutely. He never viewed the threat as a mortal one, however, and thus the suppression during his reign lacked the implacable ruthlessness observable elsewhere. And unlike his eminent antagonist Charles V, he was not a religious zealot and never got excited about religion.

At the time of Francis' death in 1547, religious conditions in France were in a precarious equilibrium. The King had not chosen to side with the Protestants, though his policy of moderate suppression had allowed their movement to flourish. With the zeal of a crusader his son Henry II sought to put an end to that. He launched a systematic policy of suppression, organized the *chambre ardente* ("fire court") as the legal instrument of persecution, but he was equally unsuccessful in his effort to burn out the Protestant heresy. The international situation did not allow him to pay one-sided attention to this domestic issue until the Peace of Cateau-Cambresis in April 1559 brought a change. Henry had every intention of settling the religious problem next, but his unexpected death three months after the Peace brought to naught whatever aspirations he may have had.

Since the heir to the throne, Francis II, was a fifteen-year-old youngster and thus a minor, the question of regency arose at once and threw the country into a heated controversy with the two leading noble families, the Guises and the Bourbons, at odds as to the constitutionally proper course to follow. Catherine de Medici, widow of the late king, ended the discussions with a fait accompli: she took over the regency for her minor son, a move which some, notably the Bourbons, promptly declared unconsitutional. This was to have fateful consequences for the future course of French Protestantism.

For almost a generation the French Protestants had experienced suppression and persecution. While they had failed in their attempt to convert the king or the mass of the people, the ongoing persecution had neither crushed their spirits nor extinguished their conviction. Theirs was a unique experience among the Protestants in Europe, for elsewhere persecution had either achieved its goal (as in Austria) or it had been brief and successfully weathered (as in England). Only in France did it continue year after year, indeed decade after decade. Inevitably the French Protestants began to reflect on their attitude toward a government that persecuted them so relentlessly. The notion that it was legitimate to oppose a ruler who persecuted the elect of God began to be more seriously considered.

Then came the constitutional crisis surrounding the succession of Francis II and the regency of Catherine de Medici. Suddenly a sound legal reason existed for opposing the ruler. The French Protestants did not exactly jump at chance, but they found it convenient to marry their incipient theological reflection on the opposition to government to the new legal situation. The temper of French Protestantism underwent a change. The non-political attitude was abandoned and increasingly Protestants became involved in the political tug-of-war that characterized the French scene. Indeed, the political tug-of-war became outright war, first in 1562 and from then on intermittently for the remainder of the century. Historians speak of the Wars of Religion, and one can distinguish eight such wars during the four last decades of the century, even though the term war is a somewhat unsatisfactory label for a generally confusing and chaotic series of skirmishes and battles.

If "war" is thus a euphemism of sorts, the same comment applies to the other part of the phrase. "Religion," though initially prominent, increasingly became a convenient rationalization for men who had other concerns and goals. The Huguenots, as the French Protestants began to be called, naturally wished for a victory of the Protestant cause, but even they used blatantly political means to achieve their end, remembering their spiritual principles less and less. Like all fratricidal wars, the French Wars of Religion were fought rapaciously and cruelly, with the St. Bartholomew Massacre of 1572 the most notorious instance of wholesale murder.

In these Wars of Religion the Protestant quest for legal recognition and establishment of their faith took a different turn. At other places (including France itself during the first three decades of the Reformation) it was a matter of persuading the ruler to accept the Protestant faith. In France, however, no strong ruler was on the scene after

Henry II. The struggle, therefore, was between two strong factions of the nobility, the one Catholic and the other Protestant, both of which sought to impose their will upon the country and upon a powerless king or his dominating mother, Catherine. Royal authority in France was represented by her, and her influence on the course of events was less than exemplary. Her unscrupulousness may have been characteristic of the age, and her antagonists were by no means shining exponents of high morality. Catherine herself possessed little religious conviction. She was mostly concerned with her sons and the future of the house of Valois. Since her sons were rather a sorry lot who combined incompetence with lack of seriousness, her task was difficult and her failure both understandable and inevitable.

In other words, religion was not very prominent on Catherine's mind as she took the country from one peace or truce of the Wars of Religion to the other. What she sought to prevent was a complete victory of either party, for that would have meant the downfall of the Valois. Some of these peace treaties, for example, the one of St. Germain-en-Lay in 1570, brought a remarkable measure of religious freedom and legal toleration for the French Protestants. France became the first country that acknowledged that a commonwealth need not be characterized by only one religion but that the sky would not fall if some citizens professed one faith and others, another.

Several "ifs" are stamped over the pages of French history during the second half of the century. What would have happened if Catherine had exhibited more religious conviction or if the Huguenots had not involved themselves in the ruthless game of power politics as much as they did? Often they were not models of otherworldly spirituality, alien pilgrims in the contest of men and armor. They may have been newcomers to the game of power politics, but they learned fast and well.

A mixture of politics and religion perpetuated an inconclusive situation—inconclusive inasmuch as neither side was able to impose its will on the other. As the century reached its end, the country was plainly tired of the episodic bloodletting. The succession of Henry IV, a Huguenot, in 1589 seemed to indicate that the Protestants at long last had reached their goal of having official support in the highest places. But those who thought so were to be mistaken. Muttering, according to legend, the words "Paris is well worth a Mass," Henry became a Catholic. His dramatic conversion may well have been another incidence of the kind of shrewd manipulation of religion for political goals and purposes which characterized so much of the era. But, more likely it was the result of his wise recognition that France, deeply divided as the result of three decades of war, would never accept Protestantism as its official religion and that any attempt to bring this about by royal fiat would only prolong futility, chaos and bloodshed. More than that, the ominous specter of the Spanish King, Philipp II, laying claims on the French throne (his late wife had been a sister of Henry III) had to be faced and Henry realized that a country torn by bloody internal strife could not successfully withstand the threat from south of the Pyrenees.

The Edict of Nantes ended this terribly confusing and bloody turmoil in 1598. Though they failed in their major goal of making the entire country Protestant, the Protestants were successful in part for they were granted the right to worship. The Edict may be compared with the Peace of Augsburg, which settled the quest for the legal recognition of the Protestant faith in Germany, for in both Germany and France every other conceivable solution had been tried and been found wanting. There was, all the same, one significant difference. In Germany the solution of the Peace of Augsburg was to allow religiously divergent territories to exist within the Empire. Within each territory, however, religious uniformity was demanded and enforced. In France religious pluralism prevailed within one single political structure; Catholics and Protestants lived side by side, not amicably, to be sure, and rather like cat and dog, but after Nantes at least peacefully. Given the disposition of the time to exact religious uniformity at all cost, the Edict of Nantes truly was a significant achievement, heralding the modern notions of religious toleration and freedom—even though we must remember that it was achieved at the point of the sword rather than with the persuasion of the tongue.

Poland

The Reformation in Poland, like that in France, presents the story of an attempt at ecclesiastical transformation that was almost successful. Protestant sentiment in Poland was reasonably extensive and relatively lively during the greater part of the century. While it was never a truly widespread movement, it was more than a mere sectarian impulse and had a good chance of bringing about a change in the ecclesiastical orientation of the land. In the end, however, it failed. The parallels with France are striking.

The customary explanations for this failure are many. It is said that Protestantism in Poland always remained confined to a minority, namely, the magnates and the szlachta (higher and lower land-owning nobility) and never became a truly popular movement. This Protestant nobility is said to have been politically oriented in the main and thus unwilling to sacrifice for the cause of religion.

While these two factors were of considerable importance, the real explanation must go deeper. A comparison with the situation elsewhere in Europe suggests that the amalgamation of religion and politics did not necessarily hinder the Protestant cause. The indisposition to sacrifice, however, is a different matter. The fact is that Polish Protestantism produced no martyrs. This may seem a curious way of evaluating a movement, but the Polish Protestants never clung to their convictions to the point of laying down their lives. To put the matter differently, unlike its French or Dutch counterpart, Polish Protestantism was never baptized with fire and the sword. When it became expedient to give up the Protestant faith, there was no memory of martyrs to arouse steadfastness. Of course, it takes two parties to make a martyr and in Poland the civil authorities were reluctant to achieve religious uniformity by force. Thus, even if there had been potential martyrs, they would have had a difficult time finding executioners.

Moreover, the absence of a Protestant figure of eminence must be cited as an important cause in the abortiveness of the Reformation in Poland. To be sure, the tracts of Luther, Calvin, and the other eminent reformers were available and provided the theological basis for Polish Protestantism. In the middle of the century when the Reformation entered its decisive phase, what Poland lacked was not originality or creativity but a spokesman of popular appeal, a man of action, a writer of popular tracts, a preacher of eloquent sermons—a man, in short, who would have translated the postulates of the Reformation into an idiom congenial to the Polish people. Such a figure was nowhere in sight. Their one eminent Protestant divine, Jan a Lasco, was tramping along the highways and byways of Europe to make his contribution to the Protestant cause elsewhere.

Still, one must be cautious in identifying the Protestant failure with Protestant weakness since the same 'weakness' prevailed elsewhere in Europe and still did not lead to the same consequences. Even the absence of popular support, while it may well have done its share to bring about the eventual defeat of Protestantism, cannot have been a major reason. After all, in the sixteenth century the common people were hardly even supporting actors in the drama and what they thought and believed made little difference really. Elsewhere in Europe popular support did not necessarily spell success even as its absence did not itself entail failure.

One must look more at the manifestations of Catholic strength when pondering the reasons for the Protestant defeat. And here the most obvious point is that the Protestants failed to convert the king. Accordingly, the central political power in the land was either neutral in the struggle for the recognition of the Protestant faith, as was the case during the first two rulers of the country, or outrightly hostile, as exemplified by King Sigismund III later on. This persistence of the crown in its support of the Catholic faith was of major import in retaining the ecclesiastical status quo. To this must be added the strength of the Polish hierarchy. Far from being deeply spiritual or even reform minded, it accepted temporary restrictions of its jurisdiction or prerogatives, but never wavered in its commitment to the old faith. It possessed the strength to resist the Protestant challenge, a fact in part attributable to the support of the king.

Above all, sixteenth-century Poland did not offer any spectacular political or social issue to which the Protestants might have attached their cause. Thus, despite its political involvement, Polish Protestantism was, in the final analysis, a religious movement, and as such it could not win against established religion. In England, Sweden, and even in Germany, the hand of the ruler manipulated ecclesiastical affairs almost at will, and in Scotland, Holland, and France unique political situations made it possible to mix religious aspirations and political goals, to the benefit of both. Poland, however, offered no rousing issues or dramatic goals.

The death of Sigismund August in 1572 brought the end of the Jagiellon dynasty. Since many of the Polish nobility exhibited Protestant leanings, the ensuing interregnum might have been an opportunity for a forceful pursuit of Protestant goals by the advocacy of a Protestant candidate for the throne. But this might have meant civil strife, and so the nobility preferred to travel the path of less resistance, go along with the sentiment of the Catholic majority and not force an issue.

A glance at the situation in France in 1559 after the death of Henry II, in Scotland after 1554 with the regency of Mary of Guise, and perhaps even in the Netherlands after the first clash in 1565 between the nobility and royal authority, suggests a parallel with Poland. In all instances a political (and at the same time religious) opposition of the nobility against royal authority emerged. This might also have occurred in Poland when the problem of a successor to the throne arose. But the Protestant nobility chose not to act. Had Henry of Valois, who was elected king, been Polish ruler for more than a few short months, the course of events might have made for a second chance. Not only was Henry an adamant Catholic who at once sought to suppress the Protestants despite the pledges he had made in the election agreement, he was also inclined to rule more autocratically than the Polish nobility was willing to accept. This situation might have precipitated the kind of opposition on the part of the nobility which characterized the scene elsewhere in Europe and the Polish Protestants would have had the kind of political issue which might have aroused widespread support.

After Henry's return to his native France came the second interregnum, and therewith the second chance for the Polish Protestants to combine politics and religion—and place both before convenience. They chose not to do so. Stephan Báthory, the new king, was a committed Catholic, though he scrupulously adhered to his election agreement, which had offered certain legal assurances to the Protestants. Stephan was a competent ruler. He scored spectacular successes abroad, interfered little in domestic matters, and faced no serious political opposition. During his rule many returned to the Catholic Church, which from then on began the period of its resurgence.

Sweden

While it is true that the Reformation was a phenomenon of European dimension, it is equally true that the countries along the northern and eastern periphery usually get little attention in the narratives of the period. There are understandable reasons for this absence of concern, above all the linguistic barrier that keeps Polish and Hungarian materials, for example, from the scrutiny of Western scholars. Still, there were interesting developments in those countries also, important in their own right and illustrative of special patterns.

Take Sweden. If reports from that time can be trusted, ecclesiastical affairs in Sweden on the eve of the Reformation seem to have been exceptionally satisfactory. Renaissance mentality had not infiltrated the minds of the Swedish churchmen and the call for ecclesiastical reform was not voiced. Still, as matters turned out, in Sweden the ecclesiastical transformation was swifter and more comprehensive than anywhere else in Europe, a fact which should give a bit of pause to those who see an all-too-close connection between the Renaissance and the Reformation. In Sweden the Reformation accomplished its goal quickly. More than that, it achieved a full and comprehensive success. It came, saw, and conquered. Nowhere did Lutheranism triumph so completely as there.

The explanation for this must be partially sought in the fact that the new theology coming from Germany struck a responsive chord in a goodly number of Swedes, especially Olavus Petri, who had studied at Wittenberg and imbibed the new gospel there. After he returned to his native land he propounded this gospel with enthusiasm and vigor, if not with originality. Alongside this reformer, however, must be placed Gustavus Erikson Vasa, who rid Sweden of the Danish yoke and was elected king of Sweden and Finland in 1523. Gustavus was one of the outstanding ruler of the sixteenth century, if for no other reason than that his rule was crowned with success from beginning to end. Though he encountered more than his share of obstacles and difficulties, he overcame them all. The achievement of other rulers may be clouded with failures and defeats. In the case of Gustavus Vasa, however, the historian can only narrate a tale of success. He lacked the flair and lavishness of his English colleague Henry VIII, but the two had much in common. They were paradigms of a new type of ruler who was to dominate the European scene during the seventeenth and eighteenth centuries—autocratic and competent, with a minimum of religious concern and commitment.

Gustavus became the reformer of the Swedish church, which he cut from its Roman matrix. When he died in 1560, Sweden was no longer Catholic. But it was not exactly Protestant either. That is to say, the country was characterized by a theological vagueness, attributable in large measure to the absence of theological controversy. After the period of initial polemic had passed, no spokesmen for the Catholic cause were on the scene to keep the fires of controversy alive. And the Protestants did not develop the dissension in their own ranks that characterized the situation elsewhere in Protestant Europe. There were no burning theological issues nor lively theological debates.

The absence of theological outspokenness finds its partial explanation in Gustavus, who was not disposed to tolerate religious dissension in his realm. He undertook a few ecclesiastical changes, enough to leave no doubt that the Swedish church was no longer Catholic, but otherwise he let ecclesiastical affairs run their traditional course. He made haste slowly. The result was a slow erosion, a gradual disappearance of things and institutions Catholic. In Sweden the monasteries were not forcibly dissolved as they were in England despite the fact that Gustavus, even as Henry VIII, faced financial problems that actually constituted the major cause in precipitating the break with the Catholic Church. The difference between England and Sweden was that Gustavus did not lay his hands on the ecclesiastical institutions to relieve his financial worries. Not that he was more generous or tolerant. He could be just as ruthless as Henry when it came to striking down opposition as in 1527 when he ordered the bishop-elect of Vesteras and the archbishop-elect of Uppsala executed, or in withdrawing his support from his advisors as in 1539 when both Olavus Petri and Laurentius Andreae, his two foremost Protestant counsellors, were sentenced to death, though the sentence was not carried out. Gustavus was more diplomatic.

At the diet of Vesteras in 1527 Gustavus confronted the Swedish estates with the desperate financial situation of the land and announced that only the property of the church provided the way out of bankruptcy. He threatened to resign and one eyewitness reported that he left the assembly hall weeping after his speech. After some reluctance the estates agreed that the episcopal castles and lay fiefs should be turned over to the King, who also was to receive certain supervisory powers over the church. Thus governmental authority in ecclesiastical affairs was vastly enlarged.

By that time the ties of the Swedish church with Rome were already tenuous. In 1523 Gustavus had sought papal confirmation for five episcopal candidates, well-meaning and honorable men, Erasmian in temperament and accordingly disposed to follow the kind of ecclesiastical policy that was pursued by the King. The request for confirmation ran into difficulties, attributable to Gustavus' unwillingness to pay the annates, though in the place of money he pledged even "greater obedience" in other respects. Pope Adrian VI looked aghast at such blatant intrusion of secular considerations into the ecclesiastical realm. Accordingly, he said no, as did his successor, Clement VII. This negative word proved to be the last direct communication between Stockholm and Rome, for Gustavus decided to go his own way, quickly realizing (aided, no doubt, by the German precedent of that time) that the bark of Rome was worse than its bite.

Nothing spectacular took place in Sweden between 1524 and 1527—nor from 1527 onward, for that matter. In 1527 came the decisions of the diet of Vesteras, but otherwise ecclesiastical affairs continued to run their accustomed course. In 1528 Petrus Magni, the only bishop confirmed by Pope Clement VII four years earlier, consecrated three new bishops and thereby assured apostolic succession in Sweden.

Within a year rebellion had broken out in the south of the country. Gustavus was accused of having introduced the Lutheran heresy in Sweden; the rebellion clearly was a reaction against his ecclesiastical policy. But it was not a serious threat to the throne and Gustavus combined eloquence and force to bring about its speedy suppression. In 1542 another insurrection occurred, for political as well as religious reasons, and this time things were a bit different. Gustavus had to scramble madly for his throne and only after a year's struggle did he finally win out. But then his position was stronger than before. At that time a number of Catholic practices, such as pilgrimages, worship of saints, and private Masses, were prohibited. Little by little, the Catholic church faded away.

After Gustavus' death in 1560 came the brief reign of his son Eric XIV, capable but unstable, a textbook case for the psychiatrist, a nonentity in the history of Sweden. He was deposed in 1569 and succeeded by his brother John, who was persuaded that his succession to the royal throne had also endowed him with special wisdom in matters of religion. He dabbled, not altogether incompetently, in theological matters, wrote two theological works, a church order and a liturgy, which sought to combine Catholic and Protestant insights and naturally evoked strong opposition from the Swedish clergy, who by that time had become accustomed to the separation from Rome. John flirted for a while with the papacy, which might have had a real opportunity to lead Sweden back into the Catholic fold had it been disposed to be a bit more broadminded and willing to make concessions (as, for example, allowing the laity to receive the cup in communion). But nothing came of the matter and when John died in 1592 Sweden was as much Protestant as it always had been. John's son Sigismund, who had been brought up a Catholic—he was already King of Poland and as such could hardly be anything else—sought to reintroduce Catholicism in Sweden. He should have learned the lesson from his father, but tried anyhow only to meet failure. In 1599 he was formally deposed by the Swedish diet.

There the story of the Reformation ended. In the early years of the

Reformation Sweden had smoothly embraced the Protestant cause, without great enthusiasm, without much turbulence. At the end of the century it retained the Protestant form of religion, though twice an attempt was made to change this. In contrast to the successes scored by a resurgent Catholicism elsewhere in Europe, such as Poland, this was a remarkable accomplishment. Still, had Sigismund shown a bit more patience, a bit more diplomacy, he might well have reached his goal.

Chapter 6

The Nature of the Controversy

To remark that Europe in 1550 was vastly different from what it had been thirty years earlier is, from what has been said on these pages, so obvious that the statement carries overtones of redundance. The specific argument of these pages has been that the vast and consequential changes taking place during that time should be attributed, in large measure, to what we have variously called the Reformation or the "ecclesiastical transformation." While in many ways an apt description, it leaves some broad characteristics unconsidered and begs certain questions.

The first of these has to do with the relation of the Reformation to the entire age: Was the Reformation of such central and crucial significance that we can legitimately speak of an Age of the Reformation? The answer is difficult—and this not only because historical labels defy rigid definitions—though the fact is that virtually all countries were affected by the ecclesiastical strife and the problem of what to do with the new interpretation of the Christian gospel was faced throughout Europe. The Reformation was not a geographically restricted phenomenon.

On the other hand, numerous developments in the realm of politics, economics, and culture had only very limited connection with the religious and ecclesiastical turbulence (or none at all), and one must be careful, therefore, with an all-too-easy postulate of the centrality of religion in the sixteenth century.

This is further borne out by the fact that the various European countries were affected by the religious turmoil at different times. In Germany the religious problem was more or less settled with the Peace of Augsburg in 1555, at a time when the French religious turmoil was only in its beginning stage. To find a generally applicable chronological period embracing all European countries is difficult, if not impossible. What can be said is that 1517 is clearly a proper starting point—and this despite the fact that the countries other than Germany were not immediately embroiled in the religious controversy. In short, we might best use a topical, rather than a chronological, definition of the Reformation, which would be defined as the quest for the (successful or abortive) ecclesiastical reorientation of a given country. Accordingly, different terminal dates for the end of the Reformation suggest themselves for different countries, making it unnecessary to place the course of events in the straitjacket of an arbitrary date.

With this definition we have already touched on one way the term Reformation is surely applicable: the empirical reception of the Protestant proclamation, the establishment of new churches, the consolidation of new forms of church life, and the weaving of all this into the total fabric of society. The term can also refer to the proclamation of the Protestant reformers, their reformulation of the Christian gospel, their sermonic and literary exhortations. Obviously, a connection exists between these two ways of talking about the Reformation. A major difference between the two is, however, that the latter can hardly be said to have been incisively influenced by the temper or conditions of the time. Naturally, such matters as the ease of publication through the invention of the printing press or the recovery of the early Christian Fathers through the humanists must not be overlooked when we search for the causes of the theological reorientation of the reformers. Nor must we neglect the fact that the theological climate of the early years of the sixteenth century obviously influenced Luther's theological development. Had he confronted the more balanced scholastic teaching concerning justification of the thirteenth or fourteenth centuries rather than the one-sided Occamism of the fifteenth-century theologian Gabriel Biel with its virtual disregard of divine grace, his theological maturation might have proceeded quite differently and his tensions with the Catholic Church would have been less pronounced.

An entirely different situation prevailed with respect to the other way we have used the term Reformation to mean the socialization of the Reformation message, its empirical manifestation in followers, partisans, and churches. In this respect, the conditions of the early sixteenth century aided the process, which would have been inconceivable without it. This is to say, that while Luther's (or the other reformers', for that matter) theology could well have been formulated a hundred years earlier, it would not have then received the hearing it did in the sixteenth century when a cluster of social, intellectual, and political factors provided a unique setting.

In an earlier chapter we reviewed the condition of European society before the Reformation and suggested that this society was far more stable than is customarily assumed and that the Reformation's success—the successful transference of a theological message into concrete ecclesiastical realities—is to be explained by the continuing presence of certain supporting factors.

The real question in any study of the religious and ecclesiastical upheaval in the sixteenth century is how a purely theological phenomenon such as Luther's proclamation of salvation by grace was so widely and successfully translated into empirical realities. But this is a misleading question. From the very outset of the Reformation controversy the issue was not solely a religious or theological one, since extraneous factors played important roles in the course of events. Albert of Hohenzollern could not view Luther's ninety-five theses as an exclusively theological pronouncement. Important political and financial considerations impinged on the matter and made him, by all odds, a prejudiced participant in the assessment of Luther's theological assertions. Or take the uprising of the German peasants in 1524/5, which indicated how easy it was to relate Luther's teaching to long-standing economic and social grievances. Then there is Henry VIII, who broke with Rome mainly over a personal problem and dissolved the English monasteries because of his financial difficulties. Even the key figure in the attempted suppression of the Lutheran heresy in Germany, Emperor Charles V, did not devote all his attention to the problem nor utilize all his resources against it, as he had threatened to do at Worms in 1521. He had other fish to fry and this diffusion of interest was to be of great significance for the course of events.

Thus, the Reformation always was a bundle of factors, political, social, and economic as well as religious. There were instances when factors other than religion were more prominent, even though the official pretense was piously religious. But in other instances authentic religious factors determined and oriented the events. Surely, we would not have expected the situation to have been different. Hordes of sinners turning into saints in a society singlemindedly concerned about religion . . . such is hardly a very realistic picture of the time. Some sixteenth-century folk may have been more religious than their ancestors or their posterity; most of them, one suspects, were not.

The non-religious factors that influenced the course of the Reformation in Europe have already been mentioned in the preceding chapter, but deserve to be recounted. The increasing importance of the ruler in the affairs of the various European commonwealths must be cited first, for this included a more powerful voice in ecclesiastical matters, even before the Reformation or in countries that remained Catholic. Accordingly, the distribution of power between church and state was undergoing a steady readjustment in the early sixteenth century, with an almost inevitable build-up of tensions between the two parties. In the German cities some burghers made a persistent effort to obtain a greater voice in municipal affairs, with a concomitant quest for constitutional changes. Then there was the struggle between France and Spain that consumed so much attention and energies during the first half of the sixteenth century.

Nor must one forget the Turks. Next to the persuasive eloquence of Luther's pamphlets the Turks were probably the best aids of the Protestant cause in Germany, and this in a twofold way. Firstly, the possibility of a Turkish attack upon Western Christendom so frightened the Emperor that he was willing to make important concessions to the Protestants at several crucial occasions in order to receive their financial and military support against the Turks. Secondly, Charles actually had to take to the field against the Turks in 1532 in Hungary, and three years later in North Africa. These occasions diverted his attention from the German religious problem long enough to give the Protestants in Germany another breather or to allow the pope to stall the convening of a general council yet a little more. Undoubtedly the course of the Protestant Reformation in Germany (and elsewhere) would have been a different one had there been no Turkish menace in the East.

The point of these reflections is that the Protestant reformers sought not only to propagate the new faith as widely as possible but also to achieve its formal recognition. In this effort they were aided by a variety of non-religious factors. Since religious pluralism was generally unthinkable in the sixteenth century, such recognition had to come from the political authorities and entailed the repudiation of the established Catholic religion. Initially the Protestant reformers may have entertained fond hopes of having their proposals for ecclesiastical reform incorporated into the fabric of Catholic life and thought. But after the harsh realities of the controversy had shown this to be an impossibility, they strove for the official acceptance of the new faith in the place of the old.

At that point two possibilities emerged. One was an immediate or early Protestant success, and thereby the introduction of the Reformation. This happened in Saxony, Hesse, in numerous imperial free cities in Germany, and in England (if here one does not apply the term Protestant too meticulously). The second possibility was a prolonged Protestant struggle for recognition. Such was the case in France, Scotland, Poland, or wherever the ruler did not forthwith accept Protestantism and officially introduce it as *the* religion in his realm. Accordingly, an effort had to be made to attempt the official introduction of the Protestant faith against the will of the ruler or to force him to make the change. Both situations had in common that the ruler played the central role.

Thus, the fact that a certain territory became Protestant meant nothing more, on the face of things, than a decree of the political authorities that the Protestant religion was thenceforth to be the official one. Naturally, such official introductions themselves said nothing about the sentiment of the people, but were acts of state with varying degrees of popular support.

That people in large numbers *did* embrace the Protestant faith can be safely asserted; this fact constituted the prime reason for the persistent impact and success of the Reformation. Naturally, we would like to know the reason for their action and those among us fascinated by the insights and methodology of the social sciences will inquire about possible patterns of this change of religious allegiance. If such a pattern of ecclesiastical change does exist, it is difficult to discern. Only one comment may be made safely: people became Protestant (at least outwardly) whenever their ruler commanded them to do so. Otherwise, the situation is rather confusing: some of the clergy turned Protestant and others remained Catholic. Some of the nobility turned

Protestant, others remained Catholic. Some artisans decided one way, some the other. In Germany the peasants rallied around Luther, while in England and Sweden they rose up in arms on behalf of Catholicism. It would be fascinating if all humanists, all academicians, all the educated (or all the uneducated), all the rich (or all the poor), all those in authority (or all those desiring authority) had become Protestant. But there is no such neat evidence, at least not so far as the general picture is concerned. What can be said is that the Protestants were generally the younger generation, outside the intellectual and ecclesiastical establishment. While this is admittedly a modest observation, it is the only one that may be made legitimately—except for the more obvious one that those concerned about religion were the most likely candidates for conversion to the new faith.

Thus far we have spoken of the Protestant effort to change the ecclesiastical state of affairs. There was also a different pattern of effecting ecclesiastical transformation. Its difference was that it sought to introduce (actually, we should say re-introduce) Catholicism and replace the Protestant establishment. In such instances the ecclesiastical labels were reversed, though in their characteristics these situations were strikingly similar. And like the Protestant quest for recognition, the Catholic effort was abortive in some places, such as Sweden or England, and successful in others, such as several German territories.

The most interesting situation prevailed in England, where Catholics engaged in a lengthy effort to challenge the Elizabethan settlement and restore Catholicism. Scholarly opinion differs as to whether this effort was formidable and ever had a real chance for success. That it existed for several decades, however, is well attested. In part it was supported by the clandestine remnants of indigenous Catholicism in England. The provisions for ecclesiastical uniformity imposed by the settlement were rather lenient. In the main, only attendance at the official services of worship was required. Those Catholics who refused to do so became known as Recusants, with their refusal as their identifying mark. Since the penalties imposed by the settlement initially were not severe, the English Catholics could hold to their faith without having the authorities breathe down their necks. Most of them were content to live and let live and sought not to cause difficulties.

On the Continent, however, emerged a different brand of English Catholicism. Its banner bearers were native sons who had left England at Elizabeth's succession and had imbibed the embullient and dynamic spirit of Tridentine Catholicism. Many of them were Jesuits, and all burned with an aggressive zeal to return their native land into the fold of the Catholic Church. Their base of operations was Douai in the Spanish Netherlands where in 1568 William Allen, formerly canon at York, founded a seminary for English priests. Allen and his confreres were indefatigable evangelists for the Catholic cause. They wrote numerous propaganda pamphlets, secretly sent missionaries across the Channel, and engaged in extensive proselytizing activity.

When Pope Pius V excommunicated Queen Elizabeth in 1570, his bull of excommunication *Regnans in Excelsis* freed all Englishmen from their allegiance to the "heretical" queen. Thereby an explicit political component was introduced into all efforts to restore Catholicism. Any Englishman espousing the Catholic religion thereby acknowledged the validity of the papal charge that Elizabeth occupied the English throne illegally. In official English eyes, Catholicism was no longer a religious option, but treason. Probably a connection existed between the timing of the bull (it came eleven years after Elizabeth's succession) and the so-called Northern Rising of 1569, which brought a serious, if disorganized, threat to Elizabeth's throne. As was characteristic of the other uprisings in the sixteenth century, the causes were complex and the demands of the rebels both political and religious. Mainly they wanted the restoration of the Catholic religion and the nobility's traditional rights. The uprising was crushed, though Pius V evidently had thought the political implications of the bull of excommunication might alter the outcome. Afterward the suppression of Catholics in England was intensified. In 1571 it became high treason to call the Queen a heretic, as this acknowledged the pope's repudiation of her authority.

The Catholic effort to convert England reached its climax in the 1580s: Jesuit missionaries, such as Edward Campion and Robert Persons, came in larger numbers; at the same time the official legal measures against Catholics in England stiffened. In 1585 the English Parliament declared it treason to be a Jesuit or a missionary priest— a sixteenth-century counterpart of "guilt by association." These outside agitators not only proclaimed a false doctrine, but sought to incite political disorder. Throughout the 1570s and 1580s the English countryside was filled with plots to assassinate Elizabeth. In most instances, the participants were eccentric and naive dreamers, and neither Elizabeth's life nor her throne was ever in real danger. In the end political efforts were too inept and the missionary efforts too limited to make a difference.

The above notwithstanding, a scheme was put forth to alter the religion of the land in close connection with a proposed alteration of the political state of affairs. Thus, the Catholic effort was the mirror image of what the Protestants sought to do elsewhere and the common denominator was the awareness that a change of religion could only be accomplished by a change of politics. Intriguingly enough, a parallel existed even with respect to the political theories drawn upon by the papist pamphleteers, on the one hand, and the Protestant writers in France, on the other. Both stressed the right of resistance against the ruler and thus Catholic and Huguenot tracts sounded strangely alike. A parallel situation led to a parallel argumentation, and this despite the different ecclesiastical labels.

The Catholic effort to reintroduce the old religion in England failed and it did so because it had no political goal. The emigrant Catholics were unable to attach their religious cause to a political issue in England. To be sure, the Northern Rebellion and the revolt in Wales in 1579 revealed a measure of political dissatisfaction. But it was limited, sporadic, and haphazard. There was really no burning political issue in England. Although on the face of things one existed, the struggle between Spain and England boomeranged and proved disastrous to the Catholic cause in England. The emigrant Catholic had seen this as a splendid opportunity and had openly espoused the Spanish cause. When the Spanish Armada sailed against England, priests were on board the vessels—and this for reasons other than to offer spiritual comfort to the Spaniards. William Allen, who had just been created Cardinal of England, had unceasingly advocated the venture, insisting that the English Catholics would flock to support the Spaniards. Allen superbly exemplified the mood of the aggressive Catholics: he was a Catholic first, and an Englishman second. Most Catholics in England, however, were Englishmen first, and Catholics second. They were of the old school, the live and let live variety, and to identify with the mortal enemy of England was for them the abomination of abominations. In a time slowly growing weary of ecclesiastical strife, their temperament was understandable indeed.

One of the ironies of the sixteenth century is that even though a goodly portion of the religious controversy had nothing in common with religion except the designation, the age showed an intense preoccupation with religious matters. Men violently disagreed with one another about religion; brother opposed brother, son stood against father. Wars were fought and men sentenced to die for the sake of religion. The graves of the victims of religion were dug throughout Europe. Most of these victims remain nameless, though the men of prominence who laid down their lives are recalled in the pages of history: Thomas More and Thomas Cranmer in England, the one giving testimony to an unalterable law of nature on the steps of his scaffold, the other casting his right hand into the flames first, since it was this hand that had written the words of revocation of his faith. In Geneva it was Michael Servetus, the antitrinitarian, who died with the words "Jesus, thou son of the eternal God, deliver" on his lips. As one bystander remarked, he might have saved his life if he had only switched the position of the adjective, for then heresy would have become orthodoxy.

It is the genius as well as the curse of man to sacrifice his goods, his possessions, and indeed his life for those ideals he deems most precious. More than that, he is willing to pursue with a vengeance those who do not share his aspirations. Sixteenth century man gave of this a frightful illustration. But man in the twentieth century is not too different in this regard from his sixteenth-century ancestor, for he continues to sacrifice for what is dear to him and to wage war against those who do not share his ideals and aspirations. The difference between the sixteenth century and subsequent centuries mainly lies in the object of this commitment. In the Age of the Reformation it was religion, the proper interpretation and understanding of the Christian gospel. Today it is something else—mainly political and social goals. The great watchwords are no longer Justification, Sacraments, Trinity, but Freedom, Democracy. The concern is no longer with the life to come, but with the life here and now. But man still has his commitments, his ideals. Man still is willing to sacrifice and to kill, to suffer and to persecute. If he were different, he were not man.

Chapter 7

The Theological Perspective

The acknowledgment (or insistence) that religion played a major role in the turbulent events of the sixteenth century raises the question as to what specific theological issues were crucial in the split between the two sides. This, in turn, raises the related question of whether these issues, as seen by Protestants, were anti-Catholic by definition, making a split inevitable once the controversy had broken out.

The answer must remain ambiguous. Some striking theological insights characterized the Protestant Reformation and we shall delineate them in this chapter. Their rejection on the part of the Catholic Church meant the schism of Western Christendom. There can be little doubt but that all in all this rejection was a legitimate one from the vantage point of traditional Catholic theology. But the fact remains that a good deal of the controversy, initially at least, concerned doctrinal matters and theological points on which the disagreement was one of emphasis and perspective rather than irreconcilable opposition. For example, the doctrine of justification was not defined by the Catholic Church when the indulgences controversy broke out in 1517, and the full implications of the relation between Scripture and tradition were only beginning to be explored by Catholic theologians. Thus, some of the contested issues pertained to a theological no man's land that need not have led inexorably to a schism. The larger setting of the controversy, as we have described it in the preceding chapter, and not the theological issues, one fears, led to the initial parting of the ways. Since the heat and the duration of the controversy increasingly precipitated pointed and one-sided statements, the differences between the two sides were eventually unbridgeable. And what had begun, in a way, by default, ended with convictions. Luther is here a good case in point. When the bull *Exsurge Domine* appeared, he could say with good reason that it was a shoddy piece of theological workmanship, since he had never taught some of the condemned propositions. But afterward he defiantly announced that he was embracing all of them as his own.

We must not forget that for a quarter of a century men of both factions were convinced that the differences could be resolved and that the common allegiance to one truth overshadowed all disagreements. At the colloquy of Regensburg in 1541 a compromise (short-lived as it turned out) was indeed reached concerning justification, the issue that seemed to stand in the center of the controversy! Only in the second half of the century—after, one suspects, the first generation of reformers who had been brought up in the Catholic faith had passed from the scene—did there emerge a confessional self-consciousness that made, at least on the Continent, for a uniquely Protestant church life. The conscious awareness of the existence of two Christian bodies is the outgrowth of the aftermath of the Reformation, and not of the Reformation itself.

If there exists uncertainty concerning the inevitability of the split, there is also divergence of sentiment concerning the basic intent of the Protestant reformers. In the sixteenth century Catholics spoke of revolution and rebellion and argued that the Protestants had revolted against the church and the apostolic faith, while the Protestants responded that they sought to reform the church according to its apostolic norm from which it had fallen. Obviously, both views were conditioned by normative postulates as to what was apostolic, and it is gratuitous to try to settle this disagreement with a historian's tools.

But both views are at best half-truths and at worst misleading. There can be no doubt but that the Reformation was a revolution. It was surprisingly little concerned about the surface of things, about ecclesiastical abuses, about dissolute church life, about the immoral cleric or the greedy prelate: that was the concern of men like Erasmus. Popular misunderstanding on this point may have given the Reformation initially a great deal of support among the rank and file of the people, but this is not what it was all about. The Reformation was a revolution, because it called for a theological reorientation. It did not so much tell the prelates to improve their lives as to tell the people to believe differently—about the church, the Mass, justification, the sacraments, and so forth. The Reformation of the sixteenth century was thus more than another of the episodes in the perennial quest for church reform that the medieval church had witnessed. The difference in this particular instance (at least from the perspective of the Catholic Church) was that something went wrong and reform turned into heresy.

Those Catholics in the sixteenth century who chided the Protestant reformers for what they took to be detestable impatience and insisted that the split of the church was too radical a cure for the ills besetting it, were a bit beside the point. In his famous letter to Cardinal Sadoleto, Calvin acknowledged that ecclesiastical abuse could have been removed without such vehement clash of conviction; he went on to say that abuses were not really at stake, but the gospel, the proper understanding of the Christian faith.

Was it then a reformation, as Calvin, Luther, and their fellows-in-arms argued? Not really, for the Protestant reformers on the Continent wanted not so much to re-form the church as to form a faith such as had never existed in the history of the Christian church—except, perhaps, in those enigmatic days of early apostolic Christianity. Ingredients for this faith could be found hither and yonder in Christian history, in St. Augustine, for example; in its entirety, however, it was new. Rather than reformers the Protestant divines were innovators, expositors of a new evangel. They themselves denied this vehemently, and the justification for their denial is to be found not only in their claim of propounding the authentic biblical message, but also in their acceptance of the ancient creeds of the church. The former showed that their teaching was not new, while the latter indicated that they were in a sense truly Catholic. The weak link in the argument was the missing historical precedent, which in its *entirety* could not be produced, even though Luther, for example, acknowledged that the faith had become obscured only during the last 500 years.

In short, innovation and continuity, catholicity and heresy, revolt and reform intertwine in the Reformation of the sixteenth century. And no one illustrates this better than Martin Luther to whose thought we now turn. This not so much on account of his superiority over other expressions of Protestant theology, but because his thought was the formulation that precipitated dissent from Catholicism. Luther's theological development is of central importance for the unfolding history of the Reformation.

Luther's theology was intensely personal. He had come to formulate it as the solution not of an abstract theological problem, but of a profound personal uncertainty. His own comment was that he had been unable to answer the question "How do I obtain a gracious God?" What he meant to say thereby was that his anxiety pertained to the question of salvation. Of course, the Catholic Church had an answer that related man and God, divine and human freedom, in such a way as to provide for the pre-eminence of God, without reducing man to a puppet. While individual emphases differed among medieval theologians, the common notion was that man had to mobilize his moral resources to contribute a share, however modest, to his salvation. The late fifteenth-century theologian Gabriel Biel, going further than most, asserted that if man *"facere quod in se est"* ("does what he can") God will not refuse his grace.

Luther's problem was that he could not find anything good in himself that he could do. He was convinced that he was completely a sinner and that his good works were stained by selfishness. Accordingly, he was stuck at the very starting point of the divine-human process of redemption. There was nothing good in him—such was his nature and he could not change. God seemed to require that he do something he could not do and at the same time condemn him for not doing it. Luther wanted to curse God who demanded the impossible.

Preoccupation with Scripture brought him to the formulation of an answer: God does not demand, but He gives. In the writings of the Apostle Paul, Luther discovered the insight that the Law, God's demand, cannot be fulfilled; man always faces God empty handed. But God wills this, for man is to give up any self-reliance and take God at His word, namely, in faith accept His promise of salvation.

Accordingly, faith became the most important word in Luther's theological vocabulary. It was the appropriation of a gift, the claim of a promise, though both gift and promise came to man in such a way as to discourage and frustrate all his hopes. Luther found the definition in the Epistle to the Hebrews meaningful, which called faith "the substance of things not seen." Luther's point was that one would expect God to love the lovable and forgive the forgivable. Quite the contrary, God loved the unlovable and forgave those who were unworthy.

Thus, Luther saw a hiatus between the external and the internal, between the ideal and the real, between what God seems to demand and what He actually offers. Even after he had come to see this as the single message of Scripture, he could not completely free himself from anxiety and uncertainty about its authenticity. "Temptations," or *Anfechtungen*, befell him, spiritual assaults, prompting him to question what he believed. In the end, however, Luther remained persuaded that this was the way God works—contrary to experience and empirical reality. The life and death of Jesus presented a significant illustration: the lowliness of the birth, the simplicity of the life, the painfulness of the death were overshadowed by the awareness that in all these God had been truly present.

No wonder that Luther extolled the life of faith, which for him was not humility (though it was that also), but a way of life. The centrality of faith suggested ramifications in virtually all areas of religion. Thus, faith was crucial in the sacraments. In the medieval tradition the sacraments had been *opera operata*, acts in which spiritual benefits accrued by virtue of the proper exercise of the rite. Luther defined the sacrament as a divine promise related to an external sign. Since the promise was related to the Word of God, the sacrament received its significance from this Word and from the appropriation of the divine promise.

According to Luther there is no other response to a promise than faith. Even as the Word is nothing without faith, so the special form of the Word, the sacrament, is nothing without faith. The promise of the sacraments must be accepted by a personal act of faith. The sacraments were thus intensely personal, especially since they personalized the divine promise, which could be felt, touched, received. The bread and wine in communion, the water in baptism, were visible seals of God's promise and they were personally received.

Luther's view of the church was another expression of this basic notion, for it distinguished between the external sign and the real matter, between the empirical realities and the true meaning, between the visible institution and the invisible body. Was the empirical institution the true church of Christ? The question was for Luther more than academic. The empirical church pursued him with relentless determination and had branded him a heretic. Had the true church so spoken?

Luther clearly faced both an empirical emergency and a theological problem. His answer followed a clue from St. Augustine, who had differentiated between the visible and the invisible church, holding that the true church was the latter. Luther echoed the Church Father by asserting that the true church is invisible. As such it is at once an object of faith.

But, although Augustine had related the invisible and the visible church so that the former was subsumed under the latter, Luther held that the two may stand in outright opposition. History suggested to him that the visible church had made increasingly extravagant claims, setting itself up as the representative of the invisible church, as the intermediary between the invisible body and the Christian.

In all this Luther's prime concern was to do away with man's religious self-confidence, which suggested to him a reliance upon externals, contrary to Scripture, which called for reliance on God. Religion was free, spontaneous, unstructured; it was to be lived in faith and trust. What Luther had to say about moral decisions harmoniously fit the larger pattern. The key words were "freedom" and "gladness." Luther abhorred strict rules and laws, and he called for free and joyful moral decisions. In his tract *On Christian Liberty* he spoke of the Christian as being a "lord over all things" and by that he meant to say that no rigid rules characterize the Christian's ethos. Moreover, no distinctly Christian acts can be established, for God has called the Christian to the ordinary and mundane chores of the routine of daily life and not to specifically spiritual or Christian endeavors. Luther proclaimed the equality of all human action—the manure spreading of the peasant could be as God-pleasing as the prayer of the monk. Not the work itself was important, but its performance. Thus, even the most unpleasant and distasteful chores—in his tract on *Marital Life* he singled out the father's chores with his infant child—assumed a spiritual significance if performed in the proper spirit. The spirit was that of faith and love—the service of God and of one's neighbor:

"Along comes natural reason, that clever harlot, looks at married life, turns up her nose, and says: 'Why, must I rock the baby, wash its diapers, change its bed, smell its odor, heal its rash, and do this and that? I will remain single and live a quiet and carefree life'. . . . But what does the Christian faith say? The father opens his eyes, looks at these lowly, distasteful, and despised chores and knows that they are adorned with divine approval as with precious gold and silver . . . not because diapers are washed, but because this is done in faith."

The implications of Luther's assertions were rich and varied. They allowed the mobilization of the ethos of faith in the secular realm. The medieval church had made a distinction between the spiritually superior works of the clergy and the works necessary for the maintenance of society. Luther refuted this distinction and allowed the common man, the butcher, baker, and candlestick maker, to perform his Christian faith in his round of daily duties. All men, no matter how lowly their work and how menial their chores, have a vocation. They are "called" by God to their responsibilities. Though Luther was always frightfully sensitive about utilizing the gospel for political or social goals, his theological understanding of the functioning of society made the work of the peasants, the artisans, the rulers religiously meaningful.

Alongside Luther stood other Protestant reformers like Huldrych Zwingli and Heinrich Bullinger in Zurich, Martin Bucer and Wolfgang Capito in Strassburg, John Calvin and Theodore Beza in Geneva, Philipp Melanchthon and Justus Jonas in Wittenberg, Thomas Cranmer and Robert Barnes in England. They were competent and conscientious evangelists of the new gospel, though few matched Luther's creativity and brilliance. To what extent and in what ways they were influenced by him remains a contested question in Reformation scholarship; for men like Zwingli it will probably remain unresolved. But even if Luther's theological influence on his peers was substantial, it never led to a slavish duplication of his thought. The theology of the Protestant reformers was rather like a coat of many colors, for individual emphases and positions varied widely. Each of the reformers propounded the Protestant message in his own peculiar and particular fashion, thereby making for a rich and multi-hued spectrum of theological expression. The emergence of distinct Protestant traditions was the outgrowth of this diversity.

But all reformers agreed on the fundamental assertions of the Protestant faith, the accusations to the contrary on the part of some against others notwithstanding. Luther was notorious in this regard, denouncing one and all who differed from him as perverse "enthusiasts" who misunderstood the gospel as much as did the Catholics. In actual fact, however, the reformers basically agreed. They agreed on the rejection of certain Catholic affirmations and principles, possibly concentrating more on certain theological characteristics of the fifteenth century than on the mainstream medieval consensus. About the vigor and vehemence of their rejection there can be little doubt; this was the common bond connecting all Protestant reformers. Whatever their individual emphases, their disagreements with one another, they shared in the repudiation of what they called "papist religion." In so doing they often caricatured Catholicism or argued from practical Catholic shortcomings to supposed theological weaknesses. But to many contemporaries their eloquence was persuasive and their argumentation successful.

The reformers also agreed that the Bible should be considered the norm of the faith. Ecclesiastical tradition was thus repudiated and this made for a great deal of misunderstanding between the two sides, which did not really talk the same theological language. What the one sought to support by Scripture, the other supported by ecclesiastical tradition. They were, as Gordon Rupp so aptly put it, rather like the two housewives arguing on their doorsteps who could not get together because they argued from different premises. The Protestant reformers assumed (almost by definition) that Scripture and tradition were incompatible. They talked monotonously about human, or man-made, traditions, whereas it was the very cornerstone of Catholic sentiment that such tradition and Scripture were in perfect harmony.

As far as the reformers were concerned, the line was neatly drawn: those who upheld Scripture stood on one side, those who clung to human traditions, on the other. In so arguing, the reformers placed themselves outside the Catholic consensus and at the same time showed that they were heirs to the particular situation of the late fifteenth century in which a dichotomy between Scripture and tradition had for the first time become an ominous possibility. The reformers aggravated the tension and proceeded to reject tradition, though in actual fact they left untouched the early tradition of the church such as found embodiment in the creeds. They were willing to consider these as biblical traditions. But when it came to the subsequent centuries, they denied that those were biblical, implying, as it were, that the Holy Spirit had decided to withhold his guidance.

This Protestant assertion *Sola Scriptura* heavily influenced the formal character of Protestant theologizing. It was biblical, as often as not a simple exposition of relevant biblical passages, with no attention paid to the scholastic doctors and authorities of the medieval church. Support was sought only from the Fathers of the early church.

All reformers were persuaded of the superfluity of merit in justification. They held that justification was a solely divine gift that could not be earned, the response of faith to the promise of divine grace. The slogans *Sola fide* or *Sola gratia* were employed to describe this notion. Some of the subtle nuances involved here were interpreted differently by different reformers and even among the immediate followers of Luther a bitter controversy ensued about the proper understanding of justification, exhibiting a zeal worthy of a nobler issue. But in principle all reformers agreed on this doctrine.

Moreover, all reformers agreed on the rejection of certain Catholic practices such as pilgrimages or the veneration of saints and saints' relics. They also rejected the papacy as the divinely ordained institution of primacy in the church. Some of the reformers were willing to let the "bishop of Rome" exercise a certain function in the universal church, but his primacy they uniformly rejected.

This point was related to the larger issue of the proper understanding of the nature of the church. Here Catholics insisted that the true church was a visible institution, organically related to Christ, its founder, represented by the Catholic Church and the supreme pontiff, the vicar of Christ, successor to St. Peter, the Apostle. The reformers, on the other hand, argued the invisibility of the true church, generally holding the right proclamation of the Word of God and the proper administration of the sacraments to be the constituting factors in creating the church. The reformers also rejected the notion of a special character of the priest as mediator between God and man and argued for what Luther called the "priesthood of all believers." Each believer possessed immediate access to God and each was to be priest to his brethren.

The Protestant Reformation suggested a new interpretation of the Christian religion. This new interpretation was propounded against the backdrop of an emphatic repudiation of traditional Christianity such as it had been known for centuries in Western Europe. Even if the Protestant Reformation had accomplished nothing more than the notion that there was a true, or authentic, interpretation of the Christian gospel which had been perverted by the Catholic Church, it would have been a dramatic achievement.

It was a new gospel that the Protestant reformers propounded, one that demanded a good deal of reorientation on the part of six-teenth-century man who had to unlearn and undo much of what he had learned and done in religion from the days of his youth—from the number and significance of the sacraments to the proper attitude to-ward the pope. That so many people were willing to undergo this kind of radical therapy shows the persuasiveness of the Protestant message.

Its persuasiveness lay in its simplicity. The Protestant reformers simplified religion by removing the welter of external rules and regu-lations, of requirements and theological definitions. To be sure, in later decades the theologians of Protestant orthodoxy could sound as scho-lastic as any medieval schoolman. But in the early years of the Ref-ormation a different atmosphere existed. The gospel according to the Protestant reformers was marvelously simple—in the final analysis nothing more than the appropriation of the divine promise of forgive-ness. When Catholics charged that Protestants only called on men to believe, they struck an incisive chord, for this was indeed what the reformers exhorted their fellows to do: to compress the full and rich range of the Christian message into the one word, Faith.

The Christian religion was internalized; it became an inward matter, a personal relationship, a trust. And this proved to be utterly persua-sive. The specific (and important) theological argumentation came afterward. In the early years of the religious controversy, however, there was astoundingly little by way of explicit theological argumenta-tion in the reformatory treatises. What there was tended to be general and consisted primarily in the assertion that the Christian faith was more simple than had been assumed by the Catholics.

If there was basic agreement between the Protestant reformers, there was also quite a bit of disagreement. Protestantism quickly be-came a house divided unto itself or, if biblical language is more appro-priate in this setting, a house with many mansions. The disagree-ments were of two sorts: the one merely reflected differing theological positions on the part of certain reforms, say between Luther and Melanchthon, while the other actually led to divisions in the Protes-tant ranks. We shall comment on two of these divisions: John Calvin, the reformer of Geneva, the great system builder of Protestantism, and the Anabaptists, the disrespectful part of the Protestant spectrum in the sixteenth century.

Calvin's theological stature may hinge on the chronology of his reformatory contribution. He was a man of the second generation of the Reformation, who attained his theological maturity when the days of storm and stress had already passed. His task accordingly was to reconstruct, to build, to organize, rather than to repudiate and to reject. It may have been his specific historical place as much as his keen mind that made him the molder of a vibrant Protestant tradition.

For this surely was his eminent contribution. His monumental *Institutes of the Christian Religion* was the most systematic and profound exposition of the Protestant evangel in the sixteenth century. And even though he wrote prolifically, turning out a seemingly endless series of biblical commentaries and a vast number of sermons, he was *vir unius libri*, "the man of one book only." For it was the *Institutes*, first published in slender form in 1536 when Calvin was twenty-six, and repeatedly revised and enlarged until it reached its final version of 1559, that established his theological fame and perpetuated it through the centuries. Calvin's historical stature is that of a theologian. By temperament he was a scholar rather than a churchman, a man of the mind rather than of action. His portraits depict this quality, the lean and ascetic face, the sensitive and piercing eyes, a man, in short, a bit too fragile and weak for the turbulence of life.

And yet he was also a man of action. Recalling on his deathbed the struggles he had experienced in Geneva, he apologetically noted that he was "by no means naturally bold." He characterized himself aptly. But when he added that "all I have done is worth nothing," he understated the case. He had done much. Not only had he changed the face of Geneva, transforming a small and insignificant town in the southwest corner of the Swiss Confederation into an important municipality, but he had also fashioned a millstream of Protestantism that rushed throughout Europe, to Scotland no less than to Poland, to France no less than to Hungary. Calvin's vision of the gospel did not remain confined to the pages of his *Institutes* but was shared by countless thousands of followers in many European countries.

Thus, in the case of Calvin no less than in that of Luther, the word became flesh. This was not merely an indirect by-product or unintentional consequence; it was planned with commitment and zeal. Calvin penned hundreds of letters of advice, admonition, counsel to his brethren in the four corners of Europe. The Academy in Geneva which he founded a few years before his death was the hub of a wheel, the spikes of which went in every direction. An extraneous factor may have helped to make Calvinism the only real Protestant option at mid-century. At that crucial time a bitter struggle had rendered Lutheranism weak and impotent. All the same, Calvin's evangel contained persuasive and congenial qualities that lent themselves to easy propagation elsewhere. Calvin was not a native son of Geneva who labored in a familiar environment. He was a stranger in the city, an alien from the first time he accidentally passed through the city to the end of his life. Naturally, his concern went beyond Geneva, especially to his native land of France. The dedication of his *Institutes* to King Francis I was a vivid reminder of his obligation and devotion to his compatriots. He was a cosmopolitan figure and this kept him free from narrow parochial bonds and made him a reformer of Europe rather than of merely Geneva.

Still, Geneva was Calvin's destiny, from the first time he set his foot there in 1536 to his death in 1564. For the first two decades he was almost constantly embroiled in controversy over his notion of how the church in Geneva should be reformed. In the end he was successful and his understanding of the nature of the church was accepted without open dissent. On his deathbed he asked the Genevan citizens not to change anything, for change, he observed, "is always evil." He need not have bothered to make the request; his demise brought no noticeable departure from the policies and principles he had so persistently advocated during his sojourn in Geneva. The persuasiveness of his work in the city thereby found an appropriate confirmation.

Scholars have disagreed about the core of Calvin's theology. Most frequently mentioned is the doctrine of predestination, which in the *Institutes* received a lengthy and masterful exposition. Calvin's starting point was the general Protestant affirmation that God's grace, rather than man's works, effects justification and his conclusion was that God bestows His grace upon whom he pleases. Thus, as he wrote in the *Institutes,* "we call predestination the eternal decree of God by which He decided what He would do with each man. For He does not create them all in like condition, but ordains some to eternal life, the others to eternal damnation." What Calvin said here was not merely that God permitted the damnation of some and the salvation of others, but that He actually willed it.

Calvin was persuaded not only that this doctrine was taught in Scripture, but also that it offered great comfort to the believers, who knew their redemption was vouchsafed by an immutable decree of God. Interestingly, the setting of Calvin's exposition of the doctrine was not his discussion of the attributes of God, but of man's redemption. Calvin never acknowledged that his doctrine made God into an inscrutable despot. Rather, by placing man's redemption completely into the hands of God, even to the point of acknowledging his divine predestination, troubled consciences could be calmed about their redemption.

Two additional features of Calvin's theology must be mentioned, even though this slights other noteworthy emphases, for example, Calvin's stress on the believer's bearing the Cross. One is Calvin's thought on the organizational structure of the church which found a dramatic embodiment in the *Ecclesiastical Ordinances* of Geneva (1541) with the famous division of church offices into pastors, deacons, elders, and teachers. In contrast to Luther and the early Anglicans, Calvin was persuaded that the New Testament offered precise instructions as to how the Christian church should be organized, and he set out to put these into practice. He also advocated a synodical form of church government in which the elders, also called presbyters, played an important role. All this meant that Calvin laid considerable stress on the external, or visible, church and explicitly affirmed that to be part of the true and invisible church presupposed membership in the visible one.

The corollary was the affirmation of church discipline. The state of redemption was discernible, at least indirectly, from the outside and a certain walk of life was mandatory for the faithful. Calvin never sought to separate sanctification from justification. The path of Christian demeanor was narrow and straight in Geneva: from the playing of cards to the enjoyment of taverns the hand of religious taboo lay heavy upon the city. This side of Calvin's activity is easily the most notorious one. It has prompted remarks about an ecclesiastical dictatorship, or theocracy, though neither term is very accurate. Calvin was never the undisputed pope of Geneva, and he had to work hand in hand with the Genevan city council. Calvin welcomed the arm of government in the support of his ecclesiastical goals, because he understood the function of government as also including the protection and maintenance of the church. The crucial issue in Geneva was not so much Calvin's effort to force his will upon the city council (this he seldom could), but the question of whether the church could order its own life without governmental interference. Notably this meant the excommunication of unworthy members. Calvin's persistence on this point meant difficulties for many years, but eventually he was successful.

In the *Ecclesiastical Ordinances*, Calvin provided for the office of the elders, twelve in number, who were to be responsible for the supervision of the lives of the faithful. They were "to keep watch over every man's life, to admonish amiably those who they see are leading a disorderly life." Together with the pastors, the elders comprised the consistory that met weekly to trade observations on the city and the citizens. Since both clergy and laity were represented on that body, one cannot speak of an ecclesiastical tyranny. The genius of the body lay in this cooperation, especially since we need to remind ourselves that there was medieval precedent for the regimentation of public life. Medieval municipalities had regimented the lives of the citizens with countless mandates, all the way from specifying the proper apparel for women of certain social status to how to keep latrines. Geneva under Calvin was different only in that ecclesiastical matters, such as non-attendance at divine services, were also subjected to scrutiny.

While the prerogatives of the clergy were thus closely restricted to the prosecution of religious offenses, the clergy did possess some political power. Thus, ecclesiastical censure for the person who abstained from Communion entailed certain civic consequences. In other words, the culprit found himself under civic censure as well and this meant that, however indirectly, the clergy wielded power other than the spiritual kind.

More so than the other forms of Protestantism, Calvinism embodied an ethos that lent itself to expression in the public and social realm. While Calvin was a bit painfully old-fashioned in matters of economics, he delineated principles that tended to point to the realm of public life as the arena in which one's salvation was worked out. Indeed, two generations ago the German economist Max Weber suggested a connection between Calvinism and the rise of capitalism, a fascinating argument, which basically held that man's economic behavior was influenced by his religious principles—though it was said that Weber's thesis had traced the rise of capitalism to the Calvinist ethos. Subsequent research has found fault with Weber on so many points that not much of his thesis has survived the biting winds of critical reaction. Most of the demurrers of the critics are well taken, for religious commitment, even of a special variety, is hardly a substitute for investment capital or competence in double-entry bookkeeping. G. R. Elton has bluntly characterized the controversy over Weber's thesis as "answers . . . devised for non-existent questions."

But more can be said and while we must acknowledge the justification of much of the criticism we should not take the basic intent of Weber too lightly. Calvin and his tradition provided an ethos of economic endeavor and behavior, conveying a religious sanctity to the mundane chores of the daily round by insisting that they were God-ordered. One gave evidence of faith not in the seclusion of the monastery or the church, but in the world, in the pursuit of one's vocation, as peasant or carpenter, soldier or king. Work was made a theological mandate and since a rigoristic ethic allowed for few elaborate enjoyments of the fruits of one's labors, all the more attention was paid to work rather than consumption. What the empirically noticeable and demonstrable consequences would have been without other factors, especially of the economic variety, is hard to tell. Perhaps there would have been none—and thus one must be careful not to put too much emphasis on this ethos. That it existed, however, and made its contribution, should not be questioned.

The Protestant Reformation soon resembled a jerry-built version of the Biblical "house with many mansions." It was never a single and homogeneous structure, but disintegrated no sooner than it had been erected. The reasons for such disintegration were many and can hardly be subsumed under simple generalizations. In some instances basic theological issues were at stake when followers of the main reformers went their own way. Luther labeled them *Schwärmer* to denote thereby that they were not level-headed men, but fanatics who dreamed up wild notions, who were unstable, very much like bees that swarm aimlessly about the hive. This perspective was normative for centuries, until scholarship in our own day and age became a bit more restrained and objective, speaking of the dissenters simply as radical reformers and labeling the entire phenomenon the Radical Reformation or the Left Wing of the Reformation.

These radicals received their theological stimulus from several quarters—among them Erasmian humanism and the medieval mystic tradition—but they would have been as naught without the Reformation. To a man they had been, at least for a while, enthusiastic disciples of the reformers and they were willing to admit that much even after their ways had parted. Two issues stood between them and their theological masters. One was the matter of timing. The radicals were the firebrands, the impatient ones, who saw no point in delaying action once they had acquired the proper insight. Since the reformers sought to be a bit more cautious, they were castigated for their compromise and exposed to violent denunciation. But more was at stake than the proper timetable for ecclesiastical change. The radicals were persuaded that they were beating the reformers at their own theological game. Luther had extolled the eminence of faith in the sacraments and had concluded that faith was necessary for their beneficial reception. He himself realized that his definition entailed certain complications with respect to Baptism, since infants did not seem to possess the necessary faith, but he found a satisfactory solution. But not so a group of radicals in Zurich who concluded that the rite administered to children was invalid; only Baptism upon confession of faith was scriptural. In January 1525 they chose to go their own way by receiving such believer's Baptism. They themselves declared that their first Baptism, received in infancy, had been erroneous, but society called them Anabaptists, "re-baptisers," and thereby labeled them heretics and criminals as well, for re-baptism was in the sixteenth century both heresy and a civic crime.

The lot of the Anabaptists was to be governmental suppression, imprisonment, torture, and even death. The Anabaptists became a company of martyrs. They were the outcasts of society, forced to meet clandestinely, persecuted by Catholic no less than by Protestant authorities. They were few in number, even though an amazing evangelistic temper carried their message from its Swiss cradle across Europe, especially to Germany and the Netherlands.

The irony of the matter was that if the Lutherans always argued that they had not received a proper hearing from the Catholics, the Anabaptists made the same charge against the reformers, claiming that they were denounced before they were persuaded, rejected before they had had a chance to defend their position. While some significant theological difference divided the two sides, a good deal of the intensity of the clash derived from the fact that neither side fully sought to understand the other.

At the heart of the Anabaptist dissent lay a staunch conviction concerning the seriousness of the Christian profession. To be sure, all the other Christian bodies shared, at least on paper, this affirmation, but the Anabaptists were persuaded that the others did not mean what they said and affirmed what they did not practice. They themselves conceived the Christian profession as a deliberate and voluntary commitment to the principles of Christ. It was not to be taken lightly and indeed, only a few would ever take it.

It is difficult to say if the Anabaptists thought of their position as a distinct alternative to that of the mainstream Reformation or merely as its proper extension. The sources are evasive, especially when they come from the rank and file of the movement, who were often well meaning but quite ill informed. But so much is obvious, the Anabaptists never shared (or perhaps never understood) the reformers' primary stress on the justification of the sinner, that insight which for men like Luther had such a profound significance—the experience that God loves and accepts man despite his unworthiness and sinfulness. One suspects that the Anabaptists showed themselves true children of the Reformation in their facile acceptance of this notion, which for Luther evoked ever a new marvel. Perhaps they did not look at the same facet of God's dealing with man: Luther was overwhelmed by God's acceptance of the sinner and the Anabaptists marveled at God's making a "new creation" of this sinner afterward.

Although the sophisticated among the Anabaptists rejected the notion of man's merit when speaking about salvation, all of them nonetheless asserted coincidentally that God had put a certain way of life before his disciples. And this way had to be followed. The mainstream reformers never voiced any basic objection to this assertion—Calvin can serve here as a splendid illustration—but they were disposed to bestow only secondary importance on it. The Anabaptists contributed the emphasis on practical churchmanship to the varied ecclesiastical spectrum of sixteenth-century Protestantism and therein lies their significance. For them the proof of the faith was empirically discernible—in the upright walk of life, the model deportment, the moral behavior. The profession of faith had to have manifestations that could be practically observed. "By their fruits ye shall know them" was surely the favorite Scripture passage of the Anabaptists.

The external sign of the commitment to the principles of Christ was the willingness to receive Baptism upon the confession of faith. The doctrine of Baptism quickly became the external issue between the Anabaptists and what might be called the ecclesiastical establishment of both the Catholic and Protestant variety. The reason is not difficult to discern. Re-baptism conveniently externalized the theological conflict between the two sides.

The stress on believer's Baptism meant that the nature of the church had to be redefined, for it could consist only of those who had deliberately chosen the way of discipleship and had received Baptism upon the confession of their faith. The true church was not invisible, therefore, as Luther had argued, but possessed empirical form. For even as the deliberate commitment to Christian discipleship was empirically discernible, so was the corporate expression of such commitment in the church. In contrast to the assumptions of both the medieval tradition and the Protestant reformers, this true church was not identical with the civic community; it was a minority, a remnant, a small and persecuted group.

Theoretically, the Anabaptist affirmation was of profound importance, since it drove a wedge into the traditional notion of a commonwealth that was at once both religious and political, and the composition of which was monolithic. The affirmation of a common Christian solidarity, such as had existed in the West ever since the days of the Emperor Constantine in the fourth century, was rejected.

In a way it was the age-old sectarian or perfectionist impulse of the Christian tradition that found here another expression. The seriousness of the Christian commitment appealed only to the handful who sought to differentiate themselves from the larger community of nominal adherents to the faith. The Anabaptists were content to go their own way, and with one or two isolated exceptions they never sought to impose their own standards on the community at large. Their principles of church discipline only applied to those who had voluntarily accepted them—in contrast to Calvinist Geneva, for example, where the entire civic community was placed under the rigor of high moral principles.

Our comparison with Geneva allows yet another comment. While Calvin was never indisposed to utilize governmental authority for the maintenance of those standards which he thought mandatory for the church, the Anabaptists practiced their discipline spiritually within their brotherhood by excluding offenders from their midst, by demanding that they do penance, by admonition. Anyone from their midst could thus take the punishment—or leave it. And that was indeed what the Anabaptists wanted. To them the intervention of governmental authority was distasteful and they rejected it, a fact that gives their position a striking ring of modernity.

Chapter 8

Catholic Renewal and Response

Needless to say, Catholic history in the sixteenth century is unthinkable without the Protestant Reformation—though to what extent this is the case has been repeatedly and heatedly debated. The widely used label of Counter Reformation conveys the notion that in the sixteenth century the inner momentum of the Catholic Church was derived from its opposition to the Protestant challenge. Catholics nowadays reject that label and prefer Catholic Reformation or Catholic Reform as more suitable alternatives to describe sixteenth-century Catholic history.

This may only be a squabble over semantics. In this particular instance, however, more is at stake than meets the eye, for the difference between the terms Counter Reformation and Catholic Reformation denotes two vastly divergent perspectives of sixteenth-century Catholic life and thought in their relation to the Protestant Reformation. The relevant question is the extent to which the Reformation influenced the development of the Catholic Church. The reason why Catholic historians show such a definite preference for the term Catholic Reformation is that they see sixteenth-century Catholic history develop and unfold according to its own inner momentum rather than to the Protestant challenge.

A more accurate assessment might do well to distinguish between two facets of Catholic life and thought—the one pertaining to ongoing indigenous ecclesiastical reform, the other to those trends that were specifically anti-Protestant in character. The former might be called Catholic Reform or possibly Catholic Renewal (to get away from the terms of reform or reformation) and its existence prior to the beginning of the Reformation has been established. The latter, in turn, should go under the heading of Counter Reformation or Catholic Response. It made its appearance when Luther began to disturb the ecclesiastical tranquility in Germany and the Catholic Church reacted against this theological peril. To renew the church and to combat the Protestant heretics: these were the two themes that overshadowed the history of the Catholic Church in the sixteenth century. At first separate, they soon interwove and became indistinguishable, fused by the struggle against Protestantism. But the two were always present.

Although renewal and response were the two eminent themes of Catholicism in the sixteenth century, the tragedy lay in the fact that in neither respect did reflection and action come at the appropriate time. Quite the contrary, the imperative of ecclesiastical reform, perceived by sensitive churchmen long before the Reformation, had to work its way slowly and tediously to general acceptance throughout the Catholic Church. Likewise, the reaction against the Protestant challenge, though formally swift and determined, lacked the thoroughness that might have grown from a comprehensive consideration. For a while the Catholic Church resembled the proverbial man looking for a black cat in a pitch-dark room; the implications and the nature of Luther's thought were not clearly discerned. The inadequacy of the Catholic response to both the issues of renewal and of reaction did its share in determining the course of the Reformation. In a way, the success of the Reformation had its source in Catholic weakness.

About Catholic reform or renewal many facts can be cited, some of which have already been mentioned in the second chapter. Not only did many bishops seek to improve the spiritual conditions in their dioceses, there was also reform in the old monastic orders, and the establishment of new ones. The fifth Lateran Council, meeting from 1512 to 1517, addressed itself to matters of ecclesiastical reform.

There was no dearth of well-meant efforts at renewal in those early years of the century. But the full force of papal authority had to stand behind them and this papal approbation was long in coming for good and not-so-good reasons. There was an all-too-brief interlude with the reign of Pope Adrian VI (1522-23), who more than any other pontiff during the sixteenth century was obsessed with a concern for the renewal of the Catholic Church. But Adrian's ineptness as an administrator, his lack of familiarity with the workings of the curia, his obsession with lagging spirituality made him, despite his spiritual sensitivity, a poor choice for altering the course of the Catholic Church. The main reason for his failure, however, was the brevity of his pontificate. Had he enjoyed a longer rule, the history of sixteenth-century Catholicism might well have taken a different course. In 1523 he instructed his legate Chieregatti to present a statement to the German diet which contained a frank confession of the worldliness of the church and the responsibility of the papacy in this regard. Adrian's words were franker than anything that had been heard from an official spokesman of the church, but they were hardly designed to win friends and influence people, for the Protestants clamored loudly that this was precisely what they had been crying (they overlooked that part of Adrian's statement which noted that Luther and his followers had deviated from the traditional faith and thus become heretics) and the Catholics felt that the papal confession had weakened their case against the Lutheran heretics.

Adrian's rule was rather like the one swallow that does not make a summer. Almost two decades were to pass before his reform concern found another spokesman. Pope Clement VII, who occupied the throne of St. Peter for an eventful decade after Adrian's demise in 1523, was well meaning and reasonably conscientious. Aside from a chronic inability to make up his mind (a quality that would have been fatal at any time), his problem was he did not share the aspirations of those who thought that the profundity of the Protestant threat called for radical policies. Consequently, the years of his rule did not bring the Catholic Church closer to an adequate response to the Protestant heresy.

Pope Paul III (1534/49) succeeded in convening the Council of Trent, an accomplishment that assures his place in the annals of the Catholic Church. He also reorganized the Inquisition, sought to effect ecclesiastical reform by appointing in 1537 the reform commission that produced the famous *Concilium de emendanda ecclesiae,* and recognized the Jesuit order. Each of these would have been noteworthy; taken together they spelled accomplishment. At the end of Paul's pontificate in 1549, the Catholic Church and the Protestant churches were farther apart than ever before, but Catholicism was surely stronger and more self-confident than it had been at the beginning of the century.

With Paul III the reformatory concerns within Catholicism, theretofore so variously but haphazardly voiced, became official policy. And as ecclesiastical renewal was made official, the reaction against the Protestant challenge became also more determined and comprehensive. It is telling that the two eminent facets of sixteenth-century Catholicism made their appearance during Paul's pontificate: the convening of the Council of Trent and the founding of the Jesuits. Both contributed to the molding of the new kind of Catholicism which emerged, its "head bloody yet unbowed" from the controversies of the Reformation era.

About Ignatius of Loyola, and the order he founded, we shall speak in another connection. It may well be that the greatest impact of the Society of Jesus was not felt until after the Age of the Reformation had passed and Baroque Catholicism was in its full splendor. But the groundwork for the subsequent Jesuit contribution was laid around the middle of the sixteenth century, when Ignatius and his "companions" set out to contribute their share to the revitalization of the Catholic Church.

The Council of Trent, in turn, lasted intermittently for almost twenty years, from 1545 to 1563, though a good deal of its history took place before it ever formally convened. Considering that it was to be a response to the Protestant challenge, an inexplicably long time passed between the beginning of the Reformation and its convening. In 1518 Luther had already appealed to a general council and in the early 1520s the German diet had gone on record favoring a gathering of the universal church as the best means to resolve the religious turmoil and bring peace and renewal to the church. But year after year passed, and nothing happened.

There were several reasons. Many Catholics were persuaded that Luther's condemnation by the Catholic Church in 1520 had settled the theological controversy and that no need for further scrutiny existed. Others thought a council superfluous since ecclesiastical reform could be undertaken by the curia and did not require a council. Also, could the Protestants be persuaded to attend a council?

This uncertainty was personified in Pope Clement VII, who did not want a council since he saw no compelling reason to have one. He made promises, one after the other, to convene a council and even went through the routine of making preparations for it. From this distance it appears, however, that he never had any serious intention of letting deeds follow his words.

Clement's successor, Paul III, favored a council and went on record accordingly immediately upon his election. But those who thought that a council was just around the corner were mistaken, for more than a decade passed before it actually convened, and this delay shows that it was one thing to wish for a council, and quite another to assemble the fathers of the church. Paul first called for the council to meet at Mantua in the spring of 1537, but half a dozen or so postponements prevented a convening of the council until at long last some thirty bishops met at Trent in December 1545, and opened the nineteenth ecumenical council of the Catholic Church. A major reason for the delays had been the chronic tensions between Spain and France. As long as these two Catholic countries feuded with one another, there was no hope that their representatives would attend a council that without them could hardly be ecumenical. What might have been a most effective remedy for the religious controversy was thus not only a matter of contention between various ecclesiastical factions, but also a political *affaire d'état*. The council was religion and politics wrapped together, as was so much during that turbulent age, and no hope existed for a council as long as the political issues remained unsolved.

This problem continued even after the opening of the council, which, as it turned out, convened at a most inopportune time. The French king refused to let his bishops attend, which meant that the major Catholic country was not represented. At least the council had formally opened.

When the few council fathers at Trent settled down to consider the agenda, they found that the disagreements concerning the purpose of a council that had characterized the Catholic scene for more than two decades were compounded by political realities. Those in sympathy with the German Emperor counseled to make haste slowly, to concentrate on matters of ecclesiastical reform and to forego for the time being a discussion of doctrinal issues which would only intensify the strain between the two sides. Others argued for a reverse order, because they believed the doctrinal basis of the conflict had to be given priority. Eventually, a compromise carried the day: doctrine and reform were to be considered simultaneously. As it turned out, however, the first months of deliberations at Trent saw several major doctrinal issues, such as justification for example, discussed and decided.

This is not to say that these decisions were made hurriedly. The range of discussion was wide, the thoroughness of the council's decisions unequaled, the competence of its participants exemplary. But the number of council fathers was small, and no inclination existed on their part to engage in dialogue with the Protestants. That the council sought to chart the way of the Catholic Church by drawing on the rich medieval heritage rather than by entering into conversation with the Protestants was indeed its most noteworthy characteristic. The decrees and canons of Trent constituted the final Catholic response to the Protestant Reformation. After the council had spoken, the uncertainties and ambiguities that may have prevailed earlier were removed; a confident and self-conscious Catholicism had defined and clarified the issues and the normative Catholic position.

The voice of a lively Catholicism sounded at Trent, one that considered the schism with Protestantism as irrevocable. The direct impact of the council upon Protestantism was slight, therefore, and Trent did not play the role in reforming and unifying the church that so many people in the early years of the Reformation had hoped for. This had several reasons. There was the temperament of the council fathers who did not consider it their task to bridge the differences. There was also the passage of time, which made the situation in 1545 different from that in 1520 or 1525. By 1545 the paths of conciliation and colloquy had been explored and found to be unsuccessful. The time seemed to suggest a different course of action.

Of the doctrinal decisions of the council two must be singled out. In April 1546 the council fathers approved a statement on the source of religious truth which held that Scripture and the apostolic traditions must be accepted with "equal reverence." This decision meant a sharp rejection of the Protestant assertion that "Scripture alone" was the rule of faith. At the same time, the fathers avoided a decision on the question of whether tradition constituted a source of religious truth independent from Scripture. In January 1547 the council approved a statement on justification. The Protestant alternative to the Catholic teaching was rejected. Justification was said to be characterized by the cooperation of man and his will with God. At the same time, sanctification was affirmed as the inevitable corollary of justification. Although Catholic tenets, such as human merit, for example, were affirmed, in general the statement was so moderate that Hans Küng, a Catholic theologian, has recently found it possible to reconcile the definitions of Trent with the teaching of the Protestant theologian Karl Barth. It is obvious that if the Tridentine statement on justification had expressed the Catholic consensus in 1517, the course of ecclesiastical events would surely have proceeded quite differently.

In March 1547 the council was moved from Trent southward to Bologna, which was situated in papal territory. The official explanation was fear of an epidemic at Trent, but really at stake was fear of the German Emperor, who had just scored an impressive victory over the League of Schmalkald and had some very definite ideas as to how the council should proceed. The Emperor promptly protested this move, which to him suggested papal domination of the council. His vehement opposition threw sufficient sand into the machinery of the council, which ground to a halt.

A political stalemate prevailed with the Emperor demanding that the council return to Trent and the Pope refusing to let the Emperor force his hand. Paul's death and the succession of Julius III in 1550 promised a new turn of events, especially since Charles' successful conclusion of the War of Schmalkald had forced the German Protestants to promise that they would attend the council. Charles chose to ignore that the Protestants had insisted on several conditions that rendered their willingness to attend quite meaningless. But in the face of this hope, Pope Julius was willing to return the council to Trent. After the resumption of deliberations, several important doctrinal definitions were agreed upon, among them transubstantiation, and the consideration of measures for ecclesiastical reform continued. A handful of German Protestants actually found their way to Trent, but matters of protocol (behind which stood basic principles) kept both the council and the Protestants from doing more than acknowledging one another's presence. The Protestants wanted the council to reject papal superiority, while the legates demanded that the Protestants accept the doctrinal decisions of the church as binding.

Before either side had a chance to reflect on how this embarrassing state of affairs could be resolved, political events intruded on the conciliar deliberations. In March 1552 the conspiracy against the Emperor of several German territorial rulers under the leadership of Elector Moritz of Saxony moved southward to Innsbruck, the Emperor's residence. Innsbruck was dangerously close to Trent and the council adjourned in a panic. The threat of a Protestant attack on Trent was more than the council fathers could stomach. But the work of the council was still unfinished and its finished work not yet confirmed by the pope.

Almost a decade was to pass before the council reconvened. Pope Paul IV (1555/59) was an ardent reformer but he thought too highly of the possibilities of the papal office to effect reform to think much of a council. But his successor, Pius IV (1559/65), was willing to convene one, if for no other reason than to avoid a schism in France, where a vigorous and politically active Calvinism presented a formidable challenge to the Catholic church. Upon reconvening, the council fathers took up the discussion of several doctrinal issues, but everything was overshadowed by the debate on a somewhat innocuous section of a proposed reform decree which dealt with the bishops' duty of residence. On the face of things, it was a secondary matter even though episcopal absenteeism had long been a thorn in the flesh of those who yearned for ecclesiastical reform. What made the matter so important was the question of whether this episcopal duty of residence was a divine ordinance or merely an ecclesiastical regulation. And behind that question stood the fundamental one of the relation between pope and bishops. The ensuing discussions showed the council fathers bitterly divided and for almost a year a radical division of the house effectively paralyzed all work.

Finally, in July 1563 the council fathers approved a relatively strict decree on episcopal residence which omitted, however, the touchy matter of the divine ordinance. At the same time an extensive proposal for ecclesiastical reform was put forward and, after lengthy discussion and certain changes, formally approved in November. Its scope was comprehensive, dealing with such matters as procedures for electing bishops, the convening of diocesan synods, and the reform of religious orders. Shortly thereafter, the council adjourned.

The nineteenth ecumenical council of the Catholic Church became history. Though its beginnings had been rather inauspicious—and the many delays embarrassing, to say the least—it had increasingly attained significance and stature. The impact of the Council of Trent upon the Catholic Church was to be profound and extensive, perhaps not so much as a direct causal agent (the first historian of the council, Paolo Sarpi, vehemently denied that it had accomplished anything worth the name ecclesiastical reform) but by becoming the symbol of a new, vital, and spiritually aggressive Catholicism, which aptly bears the Tridentine label. Though several competent and devout popes led the Catholic Church in the second half of the sixteenth century, men like Pius V, Gregory XIII, and Sixtus V, and even though the revitalization of many areas of Catholic life and thought made dramatic progress, the close of the Council of Trent marks an appropriate point for ending our consideration of the Catholic response, which is the story of both humiliation and revival.

Chapter 9

The Actors

The sixteenth century was an age of titans. It produced almost an overabundance of great men. The list of the eminent figures is long and all areas of human endeavor are represented: Michelangelo, da Vinci, Titian, Palestrina, Copernicus, Erasmus, Charles V, Luther, Henry VIII, Rabelais, Shakespeare, Ignatius of Loyola, Elizabeth I, to mention but a few. Their impact upon their own time and upon posterity was far-reaching.

We need not try to settle here the touchy problem whether men make history or history makes men. Some of the great men may well have been the product of their particular time, having been born under a lucky star, as it were, and making their contribution with a seeming inevitability. If Columbus had not sailed westward across the Atlantic in 1492, someone else surely would have done so sooner or later. No Columbus Day would grace our calendar, but the American Indians still would have been dispossessed of the vast lands of the North American continent. On the other hand, some of the titans of the sixteenth century made their contribution in such a way as to fit Jakob Burckhart's definition of the great man—one without whom the course of events would have proceeded differently.

Of this vast number we shall single out four. Their selection is not to suggest that they were the most eminent figures of the age. Rather, they illustrate four variations of the theme that has accompanied these pages rather like a *leitmotif* from a Wagnerian opera—the religious turmoil of the sixteenth century and its setting within society: Martin Luther as the Protestant churchman and Ignatius of Loyola as his Catholic counterpart; Emperor Charles V as the Catholic ruler and King Henry VIII as his Protestant counterpart. Four men, whom history calls great, each unique in his own way, yet each also a symbol for many others—together the embodiment of an exciting and turbulent age.

Martin Luther

S. T. Coleridge said of Martin Luther, ". . . not by any means such a gentleman as the Apostle Paul, but almost as great a genius." Without him events in Europe no less than in the whole of Western Christianity surely would have run a different course. Luther is one of the great men of the West, and this despite the fact that on the face of things he lacked the qualifications of greatness. He entered the public arena by accident and against his will.

His formal course of academic studies was exceptionally brief, compared with the general practice of the time, and the University of Wittenberg, where he taught, was anything but distinguished. He was destined to spend his days as an unknown theology professor at a second-rate and fledgling university. Then came his ninety-five theses and his involvement in the indulgences controversy. At once the full range of his personality came to the fore: his theological creativity and insight, his ability to discern the issues of an argument and delineate them clearly, his gift of language, his explosive temperament.

It also became obvious, right then and there, that he was an unwilling reformer and a reluctant revolutionary. He has been called an "obedient rebel" and while this dialectic juxtaposition of adjective and noun may be too paradoxical for some of us, it aptly describes the man who broke reluctantly with the Catholic Church, who wanted to be her loyal son and for a long time outdid himself with subservient expressions of devotion to the pope. Yet when the chips were down and the Augustinian monk and professor of theology had to make a decision between his church and his faith he stood firm, denounced the church and charted his own course, because, as he put it, "it is not safe to act against one's conscience." There always remained a Catholic element in him, expressed, for example, in his esteem of the Virgin Mary or his sacramentally oriented theology. Contrary to some of his more adamant reforming peers, Luther never denounced the Catholic Church in its entirety. His was a hate-love relationship that prompted him, on the one hand, to denounce the pope or the hierarchy with bitter arguments, some of which he garnered from the gutter, and, on the other, to recall warmly the celebration of the Mass or the ancient liturgy of the church. He was like the sad protagonist in Shakespeare's *Henry VI*—"O, how this discord doth afflict my soul."

If we call Martin Luther a reformer we must not forget that this was to be understood in a strictly theological sense. The theology of the church had to be reformed, that is, restored to its apostolic and biblical purity. The ramifications spilled over into the practical realm, of course, and Luther found fault with many areas of practical churchmanship as well. Important, however, were the theological implications that dealt with the nature of the Church, the sacraments, or the Christian ethos. They hinged on what Luther called "the proper art of the theologian," namely, the ability to discern between law and gospel, or, to put it differently, to understand properly the New Testament doctrine of justification.

That he discovered, or rediscovered, this doctrine was Luther's fundamental conviction. Nothing could sway him—neither Cardinal Cajetan, the learned Thomist theologian of the time, at Augsburg in 1518, nor the dignitaries of the German Empire at Worms three years later. Nor was he moved on later occasions. He always stood firm, though all the arguments in the book were thrown at him—that no one else before him had held his views and the consensus of the doctors of the church through the centuries stood against him. "Are you the only one who is wise? What if you are wrong and are heading these people into error and eternal damnation?" The argumentation bothered him, but in the end he was able to set his jaw and stand fast. Nor was he impressed by the charge that he was dividing Christendom, for fidelity to the teaching of the gospel (as he understood it) was to him of greater importance. He was a rock of certainty, even at times when those closest to him wavered. At Augsburg in 1530 when Philipp Melanchthon was in tears over the prospect of a divided Christendom and pleaded with him to consider the possibility of yielding, Luther used the firmament with its innumerable stars to express his sentiment. It does not collapse, he said, even though no pillars are visible, while man always seeks to touch pillars or "else he shakes and trembles." John Osborne's play *Luther*, with a doubting and confused reformer in the final scene, may be good drama, but is bad history. Sören Kierkegaard once remarked that Luther with all his conviction about the rightness of his cause should have been a martyr. The point is well taken, but we must remember that Luther himself was quite prepared for martyrdom.

Alongside stubbornness and cocksure conviction must be placed Luther's almost excessive disregard for his own person. Again and again he insisted that he himself was unimportant. He disrespectfully referred to himself as "a stinking bag of worms" and exhorted his followers to burn his books after his death. Only the Word of God mattered. For Luther, this Word had an objective quality—not in the sense of a literal inerrancy, but in that it made the reader the object, rather than the subject, of its teaching. Luther conceived his own role as calling attention to this message, rather like the Apostle John pointing to Christ on the Cross in Grunewald's famous painting of the crucifixion. In a sermon Luther once characterized his own place in the course of events with customary flair. "All I did," he said, "was to teach, preach, and write God's Word; otherwise I did nothing. But while I slept or drank beer with my friends Philipp Melanchthon and Nicolau Amsdorf, the Word weakened the papacy such as no prince or emperor had ever done before. I did nothing and the Word did everything."

Luther was a religious reformer who showed himself remarkably disinterested and unconcerned when it came to other matters. On several occasions he gave dramatic illustrations of this. One such time was in 1521 after his appearance at Worms, when the popular sentiment had been aroused to the point where he might have established himself as the spokesman for the German people in matters other than religion. He refrained from doing so and went into hiding in the castle of the Wartburg instead. "I could have started a nice little game at Worms," he reflected later on, "so that even the Emperor would not have been safe. But what would this have been? Nothing but foolishness. I left it to the Word." Four years later he did the same, when the German peasants arose and formulated notions that they claimed to have taken out of his book. Luther dissociated himself from them, not because he did not share their aspirations—his first pronouncement made it quite clear that he sympathized with them—but because they went about the wrong way in realizing them. Gospel and politics do not mix, he once casually remarked across the dinner table, and thereby asserted a fundamental conviction. Throughout his life he always remained strangely otherworldly. When the first talks were held about a Protestant alliance, he said that since God had protected them thus far he would surely do so in the future also.

Luther was a *homo religiosus* who had a way of disregarding practical consequences. He failed to recognize that in this world of hard realities even the noblest spiritual aspirations must compromise with more earthly considerations, though in the end he did agree to the inevitable. He conceded a measure of coercion against those whose dissent seemed to threaten law and order and allowed a limited role for secular authorities in the determination of ecclesiastical affairs. In short, he became more willing to abandon his utopian (or biblical) vision of what life and the Christian faith should be.

Some observers have accordingly thought it possible to differentiate between a young and an old Luther, the former exuberant and forceful, the latter conservative and cautious. No generalization in history is ever fully without substance and there is truth even in this observation. It must not overlook, all the same, the reluctance and pain with which Luther traveled the path he felt inevitable for his version of the gospel to receive permanent form.

There is another side to Luther his antagonists denounced during his lifetime and Catholic historians reproved afterward: his explosive and irascible temper, his vulgar and coarse language, perhaps even his mediocre theological learning. All these can be found in Luther and traditional Protestant historiography that depicted him as some sort of theological and religious Midas who turned into gold everything he touched (from theology to literature and music) is surely as inaccurate as the time-honored Catholic polemic that saw him as the incarnation of evil.

But the denunciations lose much of their validity if we recognize that some of these qualities, such as the coarseness of language, were simply characteristic of the time. Instances of objectionable demeanor were exceptional. One has to wade through volumes of Luther's works before any of them can be found. In other words, they are hardly typical of Luther; for every coarse word he uttered, one can find a hundred fine and noble ones.

All the same, it is clear that Luther did not correspond to the accepted canons of Catholic spirituality. Fasting or lengthy periods of meditation, for example, did not characterize his way of life, though the traditional charge that he was not a man of prayer has been effectively discounted. We think of him, not in the posture of meditation before an altar, but in the defiance of his plea at Worms or the intimacy of the dinner table, surrounded by family and a throng of students, eager to dispense bits of theological wisdom. As he put it on one of such occasions around the dinner table in his characteristic mixture of the vernacular and Latin: "I can drink, laugh, joke, and all that, *sed quidquid de verbo tractatur aut tractandum est* (but what is to be said about the Word of God) makes me utterly serious."

Charles V

The German Emperor Charles V was Luther's great antagonist. His rule spanned the years of Luther's public activity and the turbulence of the German Reformation. He was elected in 1519, when Luther and Eck met at Leipzig for their famous disputation, and he abdicated his imperial office in 1556, a year after the Peace of Augsburg. Between these dates lay more than a quarter of a century of persistent effort to crush the Lutheran heresy. Charles was determined to put into practice what he had said on one occasion—that he wanted to be recalled in history as the emperor during whose rule the Lutheran heresy had made its appearance, but also as the emperor who had crushed it. His pious wish was to remain unfulfilled, for no matter how hard he tried—and this he did—the Protestant heresy could not be crushed.

His aspirations, all the same, were great. In 1548 Titian painted him in shining armor on horseback, the victor of the battle of Mühlberg and of the War of Schmalkald. The artist superbly captured the self-image of Charles, who wanted to be known as a hero and a mighty warrior. On the eve of the battle of Pavia in 1525 Charles had said that he was reluctant to die before having accomplished something great. Nonetheless, his was a life in which aspirations did not turn into realities, and dreams remained dreams. And yet, how enthusiastically had his election to the imperial throne been greeted in 1519, even Luther echoing the warm words of welcome for the "noble, young blood". The first portrait in 1521 of the Emperor shows a youthful, determined face, chin characteristically thrust forward, a bewildered look in his eyes. He had lost his father at the age of six and his childhood had been colored with the anticipation of his future dynastic responsibilities. The world of diplomacy, politics, and international affairs was an intimate part of his early life. His mother was mentally deranged—once when Charles wanted to kiss her hand, she refused with the words, "You know, sire, that I do not allow this"—and his brooding and melancholy temperament must have come from her. His tutor, Adrian of Utrecht, later to become Pope Adrian VI, acquainted him with the world of Catholic spirituality, not the exuberant type often found in southern Europe, but the reflective kind of the Brethren of the Common Life. This background destined him to become a faithful son of the Catholic Church, and from the beginning of the Reformation there was no doubt about his ecclesiastical attitude. Even before he reached Germany for the first time, he had ordered the burning of Luther's books in his Burgundian and Dutch lands. He was conscious of being a descendant of the *reyes catolicos*, the "Catholic kings," and his response to Luther at Worms was that he would "act as became his heritage."

Still, Charles's Catholic piety was undogmatic. In addition to the Modern Devotion, Erasmus had influenced him a great deal. Doctrinal affirmations were relatively unimportant and matters of practical churchmanship loomed large in his thinking. At an early stage of the religious controversy this approach, if forcefully pursued, might have had the promise of success. Once the two factions hardened their positions, however, little hope prevailed that it could do so. The tragedy of Charles's ecclesiastical policy was that when he had, at long last, a chance to impose a solution to the German religious problem in 1548, the positions had indeed hardened and success on that basis was no longer possible.

About Charles's Catholicity, however, there can be no doubt, especially at the point so important during the early Reformation; he never understood Luther's religiosity and spiritual concern. In his eyes Luther was simply a heretic, a rebel against the church, who had to be crushed and suppressed. But Charles did not find the Catholic Church a congenial ally. The fault may have been on both sides—in history, as in a divorce case, the notion of the innocent party is fiction—though Charles never tired of putting the blame on the papacy. It is true that he was the only one in a position of responsibility who persistently sought a resolution of the religious conflict. Naturally, not all was pristine idealism in his case. As long as Germany was bitterly divided by the religious controversy, neither a decisive victory against France or the Turks nor the strengthening of imperial power in Germany seemed possible.

Charles, who was desperately concerned about the Catholic cause, received little support from the papacy. Different reasons oriented the attitude of the papacy at different stages along the way, of course, but basically there was always an element of distrust about Charles's doings. After all, he was not a member of the hierarchy, occupied no position of importance in the administration of the affairs of the church—and yet, governed by an old-fashioned understanding of his imperial office, he meant to settle the religious issues. This jealous attitude was very much in evidence during the deliberations leading to the Interim in 1548, when Charles not only faced the determined opposition of the Protestants but also encountered the resistance of the Catholics, who plainly informed him that he had no business meddling in ecclesiastical affairs.

The Interim was Charles's last effort. He had tried other solutions—gentle persuasion, religious colloquy, war. All had ended in failure, as did even the Interim, and the last half-dozen years or so of his reign saw him valiantly adjust to the inevitable. What must have been a painful experience for him was graphically expressed in his ambiguous attitude toward the German diet at Augsburg which was to settle the religious controversy once and for all. As matters stood, no other solution was possible short of one that assured the legal recognition of the Protestants. But of this Charles wanted to wash his hands. He authorized his brother Ferdinand to act for him and at the same time announced that he would have nothing to do with the decisions. Then came abdication.

The failure to bring about a reconciliation of the two religious factions must also be attributed to Charles himself, who had other concerns that required his time and attention. His conception of the imperial office was such that he saw his responsibilities as universal. From the days of his youth he had gloried in such aspirations. He lived in the world of his namesake Charlemagne and he sought to restore the splendor of that ancient empire. The problems of such vast responsibilities had come to the fore at the time of his election to the imperial throne, when the Spanish nobility voiced its strong objection to the inevitable subordination of Spanish interests to the larger concerns of the imperial office. At that time Charles offered an elaborate *apologia* that insisted Spain would be the "heart" of his realm. Perhaps he stayed true to his pledge. Though his first biographer, Sandoval, relates the story of how Charles was told by a Spanish peasant that he was the worst Spanish ruler for a long time, since "he always gadded about," he was more successful in what he did for Spain than in what he did elsewhere in Europe. And the situation in Spain had not been without difficulties. Soon after his succession an insurrection occurred, precipitated by high taxes, and it was put down only after strenuous effort. Charles stayed in Spain virtually for the entire 1520s and during this time he put his imprint on the land, laying the groundwork for the Golden Age of Spain later in the century. His contribution to Spain shows his abilities and qualities of statesmanship and at the same time indicates that had his self-assumed responsibilities been fewer, success might have shone more brightly.

One of these responsibilities was the repulsion of the Turks in the southeast of Europe. All had been quiet on the eastern front for almost a century, though the aggressiveness of the Ottoman Turks was ill concealed and remained a source of constant uneasiness in the west. Then, in the third decade of the sixteenth century, came the Turkish attack upon Hungary and the disastrous catastrophe at Mohacs in 1526 which wiped Hungary from the political map of Europe. The Turkish ruler was Suleiman II, a capable and dynamic monarch who yearned as much for military glory as did Charles V, indeed a worthy and dangerous opponent. In 1529 the Turks stood outside Vienna and though one can hardly say that Europeans had sleepless nights over the danger, it gave them an uneasy feeling and created an awareness of the need for defense. Charles had to raise money and soldiers and this prompted him to enter into negotiations with the German Protestants to obtain their financial and military support. This, in turn, forced him to make religious concessions and at the same time sidetracked his military efforts against France. The Protestants naturally sought to make the most of his difficulty and worked hard to obtain legal concessions. When the chips were down, however, they willingly volunteered their aid, an indication that the common solidarity of Western Christendom was still alive.

The Turkish threat was sporadic and haphazard. But it was always present—not only in the southeast, as a matter of fact, but also in the opposite end of Charles's realm, in the western Mediterranean, where in 1533 a motley crew of pirates under the leadership of Khaireddin (called Barbarossa for his red beard) offered themselves as vassals to Suleiman. Thus a mortal danger arose for Charles who was confronted by an Ottoman Empire that extended from the eastern to the western shore of the Mediterranean: moreover, Charles's lands in Sicily and southern Italy (the Kingdom of Naples) had come dangerously within the reach of the Turks. Twice Charles sought to dispel the danger, first in 1535 by invading Tunis, then in 1546 by attacking Algiers. His first attempt brought a modest success, the second spelled disaster. Charles could find comfort in the fact that his antagonist, Suleiman, was hardly in a better position and could not devote all his energies to the struggle either: Suleiman had his own France to contend with, namely, Persia, with which he waged war while Charles attacked him in Tunis. In the end Charles succeeded in checking the Turkish danger. This may not have been solely his doing, but, still, it was a factual accomplishment of his reign. At the time of his abdication the real threat had passed, even though the attacks from the East continued episodically.

More formidable an opponent was Francis I of France who made up in shrewdness what he lacked in diplomatic prowess. He, the "most Christian king," concluded alliances with the Protestant heretics no less than with the Turkish infidels to further his end and he had a way of waging war against Charles when the Emperor was preoccupied with the common Christian cause against the Turks. Four times Spain and France faced one another in bloody conflict during the forty years of Charles's rule. The encounters ended indecisively and brought no permanent settlement during Charles's lifetime even though at certain times, such as in the very first war, Charles had seemingly emerged the decisive victor.

All these considerations are important for any attempt to assess Charles V: his piety, his devotion to the Catholic Church, his tensions with the papacy, his struggle against the Turks and France. He seems to be a symbol of a complex and ambiguous age, in which varied considerations were interwoven to make a brilliant, if confusing, pattern. Charles is the symbol of political Catholicism of the kind seen during the first half of the century rather than the miiltant form personified later by his son Philip II. More so than any other Catholic ruler, Charles had been called upon to utilize the resources of his political office for the restoration of concord in the church. He tried to do so nobly and valiantly. When he sat brooding before Titian's monumental *Last Judgment* during his retirement days at San Yuste, he must also have pondered about his ecclesiastical failure.

Henry VIII

On the other side of the ecclesiastical fence stands Henry VIII of England. Naming him the symbol of political Protestantism, and thus the Protestant counterpart of Charles V, presupposes a good deal of boldness and even a greater amount of explanation. Perhaps there were other Protestant rulers during that turbulent age who deserve more prominent mention than Henry VIII, men like Elector Frederick of Saxony or Landgrave Philipp of Hesse or even Gustavus of Sweden. But even as one can hardly forget Henry after having once seen his portrait, that embodiment of obesity and self-confidence, so one cannot fail to remember him as an important figure of the Reformation. Unlike Charles, his influence was not felt in the length and breadth of Europe; Henry was an English figure only. But what he did in England he did competently, and when he died England was stronger than it had been at his succession. And this is true despite the fact that Henry seemed to be in a chronic state of near bankruptcy.

Henry's major historical distinction is that he had six wives. This is how Madam Trussaud's Wax Museum depicts him and how most people know of him. While this bespeaks his generous measure of vitality, it offers few clues for his involvement in the larger affairs of men, except for the well known fact, of course, that the transition from his first to his second wife, from Catherine of Aragon to Anne Boleyn, somehow or other led to the Reformation in England. No wonder that an earlier age made Anne the catalyst through which England embraced Protestantism or, to quote Gray's line, that Henry saw "the gospel light first dawn in Boleyn's eyes."

Henry was an evasive character, a difficult patient, as the title of a biography has it, which may well be the reason why our own cautious generation of historians has ventured forth with only one biography of the monarch. He strikes us as a rambunctious character, endowed with an overdose of self-esteem and self-adulation. What Francis I said disparagingly of Charles V, "that he wanted to be master everywhere," could well be applied to Henry, especially if "everywhere" is understood to mean "of everything." When Henry ventured into the realm of theological controversy by writing his *Assertion of the Seven Sacraments,* a competent exposition of the sacramental teaching of the Catholic Church, Pope Leo X was so impressed by his learning—or happy to have found a political ally in the fight against the German heresy—that he bestowed the title of "Defender of the Faith" on the English king. Henry had also fancied himself a serious contender for the imperial crown in Germany, an absurd interlude in the critical struggle between Charles and Francis. Theology and politics were not his only fields of endeavor, for the musical historian knows of several delightful pieces composed by Henry, and in some of the other arts, too, he made a modest contribution.

Henry's so-called divorce was the occasion that cut the English church from its Roman matrix and caused Henry to substitute a strange creature of his own, one that was neither fish nor fowl, neither Catholic nor Protestant, one that left him with the hatred of all good Catholics and the dissatisfaction of all good Protestants. Henry showed little concern for such reaction and he could afford to, for neither the hatred on the left nor the dissatisfaction on the right constituted a formidable threat. The only serious challenge of his rule, the Pilgrimage of Grace, was put down by him with a shrewd combination of force and dishonesty. Individual dissenters—orthodox Catholics one day and committed Protestants the next—were sent to the gallows or to the stake with the same gesture. Men of such differing commitment as John Fisher, Thomas More, Robert Barnes, or Thomas Cromwell suffered a common martyrdom at the hands of a ruthless king. And he was as ruthless as he was sensuous. He could change confidants and advisors like a shirt. When a man had served his purpose—such as Cardinal Wolsey in 1529 or Thomas Cromwell eleven years later— he lost the King's favor and sometimes his head. They were tools in his hands, to be thrown away when they were no longer needed. The exception was Thomas Cranmer, the former Cambridge don, who had first gained the king's attention by suggesting that the universities of Christendom be consulted concerning the royal divorce and who had afterward been elevated to the archepiscopacy of Canterbury. Cranmer served his King for almost two decades, completely untying the legal knots of one Henrician marriage after the other and obediently administering ecclesiastical affairs in accord with Henry's wishes. That Cranmer was a staunch Protestant—and became even more so as time passed—and still got along so well with the theologically conservative King, presents something of a puzzle and suggests that he might have been an opportunist. Fortunately, he never outlived his usefulness to the King and this, perhaps, because he was never of crucial import in the first place. One of the King's undisputed abilities (and it was a brilliant one indeed) was his uncanny selection of competent advisors: when it came to picking the right man for the right place, no one did it better than he. Henry knew how to listen and he always heard the right tune. His reaction to Cranmer's proposal concerning a consultation of the universities is a good case in point, for no matter how futile, it was a good suggestion.

The great statesman is not necessarily one who both conceives an idea and translates it into action, but one who picks the best idea, be it his own or that of one of his advisors, and translates that into action. Henry had two advisors for the greater part of his reign who were, though in many ways quite dissimilar, both distinguished by competence: Cardinal Wolsey and Thomas Cromwell. During the former's period of power the eminent consideration was foreign policy, though Henry, young, handsome, vigorous, was preoccupied with activities becoming these qualities. Wolsey could run the show, even to the point of thinking of himself as *alter rex* (Hampstead Court which he built is a telling symbol of his grandiose aspirations), though Henry periodically reminded him who really was master in the house. But when the Cardinal failed to deliver the divorce to the King, the reaction was swift and the royal disgrace inevitable. Cromwell, not drunk with the arrogance of power and the ostentatiousness of luxurious living, possessed a different temperament and pursued his purposes differently. During the 1530s the overriding issues in England were ecclesiastical ones. This included the use of Parliament for their resolution and Cromwell worked masterfully through administrative changes and legal statutes.

This takes us to the religious policy of the King, aside from his multiple marital machinations, the major characteristic of his rule. That he made England Protestant did not entail religious originality. Still, it was an intriguing solution to reject only papal supremacy and leave the remainder of the English Church intact. Practically, Henry only executed the policies proposed by Cromwell. But without Henry's alteration of ecclesiastical affairs, no matter how contradictory it was, the reformatory efforts under Edward and Elizabeth would have been neither possible nor successful.

Henry himself was a good Catholic, except at the point of papal supremacy. But inasmuch as that point embodies the essence of the Catholic faith, calling him a Catholic may not be too meaningful. On the face of things, however, Henry embraced Catholic doctrine from beginning to end, from the time he earned his theological spurs with his literary pronouncement against Luther to the time he sought to stabilize the religious situation with the Six Articles Act of 1539, which remained in effect (at least on paper) for the remainder of his reign.

Henry was fond of displaying his theological learning and he did so on any number of occasions, for example, in state documents, in the drafting of the Six Articles or the *King's Book*.

Still, the whole matter remains enigmatic. One must also consider the dissolution of the monasteries, the introduction of an English Bible, and the injunctions of the late 1530s: all more or less distinctly Protestant policies. Moreover, a Protestant was tutor of Henry's son Edward and the proposed council of regency for Edward, while excluding the staunch Protestants as well as Catholics, leaned toward Protestant sentiment and left little doubt about a Protestant course during Edward's minority.

But what could Henry do? In the eyes of the Catholic Church his son was the offspring of an illegitimate union and Henry saw clearly that any reintroduction of Catholicism in England was bound to have serious repercussions. Perhaps that unscrupulous, shrewd, and vicious King did possess some religious conviction after all, which prompted him to pursue a conservative policy during his own reign, but compelled him to see the necessity for a Protestant policy afterward if his work was to survive.

The English Reformation was unique and had no parallels anywhere in Europe. To be sure, the political ruler's shrewd manipulation of ecclesiastical affairs was commonplace and we must not single out Henry for credit (if such be the proper word) where it is not due. All over Europe rulers were imposing their will upon their subjects and the theologians as the *ultima ratio* of the theological controversy. Henry only followed precedent and showed thereby, in yet another way, his amazing ability to learn from others. The uniqueness of the English situation lies in the fact that the ecclesiastical transformation occurred without a stringent religious rationale. It was not that England remained Catholic or turned Protestant because its king was himself Catholic or Protestant. Rather, England changed its formal ecclesiastical allegiance because its king found it politically and dynastically convenient to do so. To be sure, there were English reformers, men who diligently sought to establish the true biblical religion in England. But when all was said and done, these theologians, churchmen, and academicians never decisively oriented the course of events. Despite—or even because of—their presence, England is as splendid a case for a political Reformation as one can find anywhere in the sixteenth century. And Henry VIII was its competent, proud, and arrogant architect.

Ignatius of Loyola

If any Catholic churchman in the sixteenth century is to be singled out for recognition, it must be St. Ignatius of Loyola. He is the other great anti-Luther of the sixteenth century and his canonization by the Catholic Church bespeaks his significance during that eventful century.

Like Luther, Ignatius came to be a churchman through a personal crisis, though in his case it was (at least on the face of things) a bit more dramatic and spectacular—a conversion on his sickbed after he had lived the turbulent and somewhat rowdy life of an army officer. Unlike Luther, however, he found the answer to his spiritual problems within the bosom of his church, whose answers he never questioned. Perhaps his Spanish environment provided him with a different spirituality than Luther experienced in Erfurt or Wittenberg. Perhaps his problem was of a simpler sort, for the helps he turned to were hardly sophisticated: a *Life of Christ*, a collection of stories about saints, a few devotional books.

Ignatius signifies that the Catholic Church could still offer spiritual solace and comfort to man in the sixteenth century. We woefully misinterpret the situation of that time if we take Luther's circumstances as typical; they were not. In Ignatius' case, the Catholic Church seemed bent on disappointing and testing him, thwarting his intention to serve it at every turn of the way. He was prevented from staying in Palestine, had brushes with the Inquisition, and even was incarcerated. He encountered staunch ecclesiastical opposition to the Society of Jesus, which later was to help the church at a time of dire need. Most would have given up in frustration and despair. Ignatius persisted, for he was persuaded that there was a difference between his apparent defiance and the reality of his devotion. In later years he penned reflections on *The Mind of the Church* and noted in them that "to arrive at complete certainty, this is the attitude of mind we should maintain: I will believe that the white object I see is black if that should be the decision of the hierarchical church." Ignatius shared the core of the Catholic faith: the notion that the empirical church stands in unbroken continuity with the apostolic church and in organic union with Christ, its head.

Ignatius's religiosity was that of a mystic. From his early days at Manresa to his final years at Rome a mystic quality characterized his spiritual life. It was not the mysticism that envisioned the soul as the spouse of God or Christ; it was trinitarian and eucharistic. Ignatius spoke of "insights" and his visions were of an "understanding" sort that allowed him to penetrate, for example, the mysteries of the trinity, "perceiving the one essence as in a lucid clarity." Such illuminations explained the Christian faith to him. His visions were seen through a mist of tears, the tears that he believed to be outward manifestations of divine grace. Again and again in his writings he made reference to the tears that flowed, sometimes several times a day, sometimes so vehemently that they prevented him from speaking, sometimes so profusely that the doctor ordered him not to weep anymore. This may have been the result of a body that was weakened by extensive fasts and of an hyperemotional temperament that could not control itself. One can easily think of a natural explanation, of course, though those standing in the tradition that nurtured Ignatius will be disposed to look for different explanations.

During the first years after his conversion Ignatius experienced considerable uncertainty over his spiritual vocation, alternated between desolation and consolation. It has been said of Pope Julius III that he wanted to storm heaven by force, and one might well say of Ignatius that at Manresa he wanted to storm heaven by asceticism. He spent hours at a time in prayer, lived on alms, fasted extensively, flagellated himself, neglected the care of his body. He consulted others about spiritual matters, to discern if his direction was the same as theirs. He overcame his own uncertainties when he began to stress service in addition to penance and the depth of the interior life in addition to the apostolic zeal. Ignatius was persuaded that at Manresa he had received the fullness of spiritual insight. Whatever understanding he had received later "did not come up to as much as those he received at that one time."

Ignatius was not a great theologian, even though he was an eminent light in the sixteenth-century ecclesiastical firmament. Tellingly, one of his associates spoke of his "limited endowment of eloquence and learning." He is not really remembered for any thorough or brilliant theological treatise. He wrote extensively; his words, however, were not words of theological exposition or erudition, but words of counsel and exhortation. His style was heavy, cumbersome, difficult. The reader can seldom avoid the feeling that the writer must have thought the world moved by forces other than the printed word.

Ignatius was a man of action. This is what he had been as a soldier and this is what he continued to be as a churchman. It is no coincidence that the literary document for which he is best known, the *Spiritual Exercises,* was a book of action rather than reflection and meditation.

And in this sense the period from 1540 to 1556 was the most important one in his life, for then he found it possible to put his natural endowments to the use of the church, guiding the Society of Jesus through its initial history. He was a born leader, a born organizer, and a man of intense determination and will power. He overcame all the obstacles and hindrances and he labored until his creation, the Society of Jesus, had become a powerful instrument in the hands of the Catholic Church.

Ignatius began to work on that famous handbook of spiritual edification, the *Spiritual Exercises*, soon after his conversion. As its title indicated, it was not a devotional book in the customary sense of the word. The reader was to be more than a reader; he was to be a doer. Detailed spiritual exercises to be followed for four weeks were to bring purification of the soul. The genius of this little book lay not so much in its content as in its form, its regimentation, its discipline. Nothing was left uncertain; everything was clearly specified and delineated. Ignatius' military background helped to mold the *Exercises*, for he who had known the value of discipline on the battlefield of armies was persuaded of the value of discipline on the battlefield of the soul.

Ignatius' genius for administration and his commitment to the things of the spirit lay behind the Society of Jesus. The Society was his work and creation; he formed it according to his insights and his propensity. From the beginning of his spiritual pilgrimage he had sought to transplant his own enthusiasm to others. At Alcala, Salamanca, and at Paris he had gathered a handful of committed souls around him, had given them the *Exercises* and exhorted them to spirituality. In the beginning his experiences were disappointing and the price he had to pay for them was high. Few were prepared for the intensity of commitment which he sought and the physical rigor necessary to take the *Exercises* was formidable.

Eventually he scored a measure of success. Numerically, it was nothing spectacular, though numbers can here hardly convey the significance of the accomplishment. After several years in Paris, Ignatius had gathered six "companions" and on August 15, 1534, these men pledged themselves to service to the Catholic Church and the Pope. Soon they were joined by three others, and still others joined later. This was the handful of men who formed the beginning of the Society of Jesus. The Catholic Church has raised to the honors of the altar no less than six of the early Jesuits, a persuasive acknowledgment of its esteem of their work and life.

The imprint of Ignatius was on all these men. His spirituality, his vision, his commitment had not only brought about the Society but had also molded the piety of its members. Naturally, the Jesuit saints exhibited their own particular traits of character and qualities of spirituality. But they had received their common stimulus from Ignatius, whom they tellingly called "father." The formal means had been the *Exercises,* used by Ignatius to deepen the spirituality of others; the informal means was the personal contact. Ignatius successfully communicated his own vision of the spiritual life to others. More than that, he translated his own spirituality into an empirical form. The Society of Jesus was an extension of Ignatius, his shadow—if ever a group of men can be but the shadow of another.

The formal structure of the Society was embodied in the Constitutions of 1539. These were characterized by unique features, such as the dispensation from saying the canonical hours. Spiritual commitment on the part of the members of the Society was presupposed (something other orders made an end in itself), and they strove to utilize it for the good of the church. The Jesuits were consciously other-directed as well as explicitly church-oriented. They took their own spirituality for granted or worked on it on the side through the *Spiritual Exercises* while they devoted their energies and their talents to the strengthening of the church. The Jesuits were like soldiers in a tactical exercise, directed by the general of the Society. If some monastic orders had sought individual spiritual edification and others had striven for a judicious mixture of cultivating the members' spirituality and works of charity or edification, the Jesuits went all out in their efforts for the church.

The requirements for membership were stringent. Ignatius knew that a few well trained soldiers were superior to a huge throng of incompetent ones. Numerically the Jesuits were insignificant and by no means a "mighty army." But they combined competence and dedication—and they were always at the right place at the right time. Their significance was most pronounced in the second half of the century, the time ordinarily associated with the term Counter Reformation, for then their relentless pursuit of ecclesiastical vitalization aided in a slowing down of the Protestant advances at places such as Germany, Hungary, Poland.

This was the legacy of the man who may well have been the greatest of all sixteenth-century Catholics, he who signed all his letters with "poor in goodness, Ignatius."

Chapter 10

The Significance of the Age

The most obvious consequence of the Reformation was, of course, the split of Western Christendom into several parochial bodies. No longer was the Christian Church one: it was many—at first two, then three, four, five, and even six bodies that offered different interpretations of the Christian faith, each claiming to be its sole and authentic interpreter. And even though they persuaded only themselves, and not one another, collectively they exhibited a hopeless and chaotic incompatibility that could not help but lessen the general Christian claim for the possession of truth.

The bearing of these intra-Christian feuds, strifes, and squabbles on the course of events in the seventeenth and eighteenth centuries was profound indeed. At the same time this splintering meant a diversification of Christian history, which became complex as it divided into different streams and separate traditions. And since these traditions established themselves within political boundaries, Protestant countries saw an increasing significance of the territorial ruler. Henry VIII had realized this when he followed Thomas Cromwell's suggestion that England was an empire, a self-contained commonwealth where no outside power might interfere. His somewhat arrogant title "supreme head of the church" expressed this eminent position of a political ruler superbly.

In the Protestant territories in Germany the ruler became the "Notbischof," or "emergency bishop," which lacked the dramatic confidence of the English title, but as a practical matter was not too different. The breaking up of the huge monolithic body of Catholicism into national fragments meant a redistribution of power between the ecclesiastical and the political authorities. A new relationship between the political and the ecclesiastical authorities began to characterize the scene, though the traditional alliance of what a later age called "throne and altar" continued as theretofore. There was no separation of church and state and to be a citizen automatically meant being a member of the Christian church officially accepted in the realm. At the same time, theological deviation entailed civic repercussions. This characterized the state of affairs after the Reformation as much as it had before. And yet a change did take place inasmuch as the role of the political authorities increased. More and more rulers tended to determine the course of ecclesiastical affairs and sought to put their stamp of approval on the exercise of religion.

The picture would not be complete, however, without the recognition that the Protestant reformers introduced a new facet by their theological reformulation of the relation between temporal and spiritual power. Luther, for one, wanted the two to be separate, but he was willing to think of the ruler as "emergency bishop," a temporary concession based upon the practical necessities of the situation. Calvin envisioned a distinctly Christian commonwealth in Geneva and never was slow to use the arm of government to achieve his religious goals. Nonetheless, he clearly circumscribed the authority of government in the "internal affairs of the church." The fact that the church was no longer one universal body encompassing the breadth and width of Europe, but several small and geographically restricted bodies, meant that there was neither moral authority nor practical power to impose the ecclesiastical will upon the state.

This situation had consequences for both toleration and religious liberty. Part of the significance of the Reformation was that these principles, theretofore unheard of, found several forceful spokesmen. First among the reformers to assert that "to burn heretics is against the Holy Spirit," (the bull *Exsurge Domine* disagreed!) Luther pointed to the futility of combatting ideas with fire and sword. As the years passed he and the other reformers became a bit less outspoken in this matter and acknowledged that inasmuch as theological deviation entailed disastrous consequences for public law and order it was proper to suppress it by force and governmental fiat. On the basic principle, however, they never shifted ground and thus provided a base for more outspoken men to present the case. The eloquent spokesmen for religious liberty were outsiders, men such as Sebastian Franck or Sebastian Castellio, who held that faith could not be coerced and that, moreover, most of the theological issues contested between the various ecclesiastical factions were of secondary importance. Only the basic affirmations of the Christian faith mattered and minor deviations could be overlooked.

But the age preferred to be narrow-minded and sought religious uniformity, often with fire and sword. Those who defiantly advocated religious freedom constituted a minority and their case was a hopeless one. Still, at no time in the history of the West had the banner of religious freedom been raised so vigorously and while a century was to pass before the dream of Franck, Castellio, Acontius, Postel, and others became reality, their thought aided in the dissolution of a notion that had dominated Western Christendom for almost a millennium.

One of the ironies of the Reformation was that after decades of intense religious and ecclesiastical preoccupation, the hold of religion on European society was less formidable than it had been when the controversy began. To be sure, in a variety of ways religion continued to be at the very center of society. But by the end of the age a second culture had emerged, one that was neutral toward traditional religion and preferred to go its own course. In 1600 Europe undoubtedly was more worldly than it had been one hundred years earlier.

Even for the Reformation era the case must be stated modestly. No matter how preoccupied sixteenth-century man was with religion, he did other things but spend every waking moment pondering the things of the spirit. Indeed, some of the things he ostensibly did *ad majorem Dei gloriam* turned out to have some definite non-religious consequences. The dissolution of the monasteries in Protestant lands, for instance, meant a large-scale redistribution of real estate. By the same token, certain purely secular developments had indirect religious ramifications. Take the discoveries, for example, which first broadened the horizon of Europe in the closing decades of the fifteenth century and increasingly added new lands and peoples onto the map. While the full impact of these discoveries was long in coming, it did bring about a departure from various traditional notions. The confrontations with new religions posed a challenge to the Christian religion, and geographic and cultural extension of the world entailed an awareness that the Bible was not necessarily a guide in all areas of human endeavor.

The same held true for certain scientific advances. In the main, the sixteenth century was not what we might call scientifically minded, though any history of Western science will include enough names such as those of the Belgian Andrea Vesalius and his treatise *On the Structure of the Human Body* to show that empirical investigation became more and more widespread. Undoubtedly the major event was the publication of Copernicus' *On the Revolution of the Heavenly Bodies*. When this book appeared in 1543 it included a preface by Andreas Osiander, the reformer of Nuremberg, who stressed the need for hypotheses in the realm of scientific investigation. But such quasi-official ecclesiastical endorsement of daring scientific propositions did not prevent extensive theological misgivings about the novel views propounded, which seemed to clash with the traditional reading of Holy Writ. The first skirmish in the war between religion and science began. But it did so rather inadvertently, for we must remember that in the sixteenth century the evidence in support of the Copernican hypothesis was fragmentary and the case by no means as ironclad as a century later when Galilei with the help of a polished piece of glass destroyed the old world view once and for all. In the sixteenth century the scientific establishment was as much against fancy new ideas as were the theologians whose opposition was understandable. But the fateful discrepancy between the traditional reading of the Bible and the insights of the scientists had begun.

The arts and literature were also changing in the sixteenth century, in some measure reflecting the religious orientation of the age. Some of the eminent artistic achievements of the age were religious in nature and this characterization applies to those of Catholic men of the arts no less than to those of Protestant ones. The desire to express religious conviction and commitment in artistic form was no respecter of ecclesiastical traditions. Among those who owed their allegiance to the Catholic Church were men like Michelangelo (1475-1564), Titian (c. 1490-1576), or Tintoretto (1518-1594), whose work showed a transition from secular motifs to religious ones. Michelangelo's "Pietà" expressed this no less than Tintoretto's "Presentation of the Virgin in the Temple." A deep religiosity was found in the work of these men, who used new forms and techniques to express it. No longer did an obvious piety speak from the canvases and statues, with eyes turned heavenward and haloes. Color and dynamic motion were utilized to express the spiritual aspirations of the artist and his subjects. This was not much different among the artists whose allegiance was to the new faith. We can bypass the numerous third-rate artists, fortunately never recalled in the history of art, men who used their modest talents mainly for blatant propaganda efforts. Of the better known figures, we note men like Lucas Cranach (1472-1553), in his creativity hardly the equal of his eminent Italian contemporaries, but nonetheless an indefatigable champion of the Protestant cause who also could be quite secular, as, for example, in his "Judgment of Paris" with its three coquettish nudes who posed quite a challenge for the bearded and aged Paris.

One must not overstate the case. The religious mood that permeated much of the pictorial arts was by no means the only one. Pieter Brueghel's peasant canvases, for example, conveyed an earthiness seemingly devoid of religiosity, though his work may be viewed differently and in a theological sense, in which case his portrayals of peasants depict human frailty and weakness, pictorial representations of what might be called his implied theology. One suspects that the Dutch artist would have been surprised at the theological meaning put into his work. When he did pick occasional biblical themes, such as in his "The Blind Leading the Blind," he offered what seemed to be a satirical commentary on the religious strife of the day rather than a deeper religious yearning.

There were other and more obvious instances of secular art: Correggio's "Jupiter and Io" with its portrayal of physical ecstasy, or Parmigianino's "The Madonna with the Long Neck," unreal in its portrayal of the human form—a notion of ethereal beauty rather than spirituality. Later in the century Paolo Veronese painted "Christ in the House of Levi" in a completely naturalistic setting, depicting an elaborate though stilted banquet and, as the Inquisition charged him, showing Christ with "buffoons, drunkards, Germans, dwarfs and the like."

Literature exhibited the same ambivalence between the religious and the secular. In sheer quantity—and perhaps in quality as well—the theological and religious works dominated the scene. The great books of the time (great in terms of the impact they made upon the contemporary scene) were the tomes emerging from the theological combat, foremostly the writings of the Protestant reformers, of course, but also those of the Catholics. The Protestant reformers were eloquent men of letters and in part their success was derived from their ability to turn a smooth and persuasive phrase. We need not say much about their literary contribution. They utilized the vernacular language and made it a splendid vehicle of communication. They took the theological controversy to the people and thereby stimulated the preoccupation with the language of the people. In each country a vernacular Bible marked an important milestone in the history of the Reformation. It was spearheaded by Luther's German Bible, of course, but England, Denmark, Sweden, France, Poland, Hungary followed the German precedent and produced vernacular Bibles of their own. This use of the vernacular helped to make the Protestant cause successful.

With the exception of some obvious propaganda pieces that came from the printing presses in the early years of the Reformation, there were few attempts to use a secular medium to convey a religious message. The eminent work which is both good religion and great literature —one thinks of Milton's *Paradise Lost,* for example—is unknown in the sixteenth century. The Reformation, while producing a vast religious literature, influenced the genuine literary development only indirectly at best.

In the realm of music the impact of the Reformation was pronounced, and this for the simple reason that here a direct connection existed with the liturgical life of the church. The reactions to new theological trends or religious commitments could find easy and appropriate expression, quite in contrast to the arts and literature where the connection could never be more than indirect.

The Reformation was a singing movement. Luther set the tone by writing and composing a fairly large number of hymns—among them his famous "Mighty Fortress," the "Marseillaise of the Reformation"— though the Protestant tradition represented by Zwingli and Calvin failed to share this enthusiasm for church music. In Zurich the organs were destroyed and congregational singing discontinued for most of the century. Calvin himself thought highly of congregational singing but otherwise had little use for music in worship.

Aside from the occasional use of secular melodies and a preference for biblical texts in the vernacular, however, one can hardly speak of a distinctive Protestant church music in the sixteenth century. What proved to be characteristically Protestant came only at a later time. In the early decades of the Reformation the ear alone could notice little, if any, difference between Protestant and Catholic church music.

In the long run, however, the Reformation exerted considerable influence on music. The secularization of education created Protestant school teachers who were able to go about their task of writing and teaching music unburdened by the rigidity of the Catholic musical tradition. Though most of them were mediocre in competence and limited in outlook, they created a musical expression which in the seventeenth century reached significant heights. It was then that the impact of the Reformation was felt and a distinctly Protestant musical tradition, exemplified by the motets and passions of such composers as Herman Schein and Heinrich Schutz, made a lasting contribution.

The musical development followed the pattern of literature and the arts: a general trend continued, but was modified by the Reformation. Polyphony scored its victory and the musical titans of the age, Orlando de Lassus, Palestrina, Giovanni Gabrieli, took to the new musical forms like fish to water and used them to compose works congenial to the temper of the church: Lassus' *Le Lagrime di San Pietro*, Palestrina's *Missa Papae Marcellae*, Gabrielli's *In Ecclesiis* are good illustrations. William Byrd, a devout Catholic in Elizabethan England, wrote: "I have learned that there is such a profound and hidden power in those words [of Scripture], that to one thinking on things divine, pondering them with diligent and earnest concentration, all the most fitting melodies come as it were of themselves."

In sum, the artistic development in the sixteenth century brought a continuing preoccupation with religious themes. Religion, the Bible, the Christian tradition, continued to be the primary subject matter for the artists. Indeed, the religious involvement of the age intensified this orientation and some artists expressed in their work the impact of the religious controversy on their artistic vision. In a larger sense, however, the Reformation failed to bring about a dramatic religious preoccupation of the arts, especially since the preponderance of religious themes in earlier epochs may well have been (in part at least) sociologically, rather than ideologically, conditioned. This is to say that the church was virtually the only patron of the artist, for his paintings, sculptures, or musical compositions. Naturally, the themes chosen were religious ones. Only with the emergence of new kinds of patrons, the political rulers or the prosperous burghers in the towns, did this limitation disappear.

In the sixteenth century, the broader evolution of painting, sculpture and the graphic arts, so dramatically evidenced by the Renaissance, continued as the artist discovered nature, man, and motion. As often as not, it is the canvas of any landscape, of any group of blind men, of any banquet, of any woman that the artist wanted to put before his viewers rather than explicitly spiritual or religious themes. While this may be called the Protestant doctrine of "vocation," which held that religious faith could be expressed in non-religious endeavors, it did mean the strengthening of a trend that in the end led to the secularization of the arts.

Our comments on the significance of the Reformation for the arts take us to the problem of the relationship between the Reformation and the Renaissance, whose chronological simultaneity begs for explanation. The suggestion has been made that the Reformation was the religious expression of the Renaissance and on the face of things this seems to have much to say for itself. The two movements shared a common reaction against the arid forms of medieval life and a stress on the individual. One might even speak of the "two reformations in the sixteenth century," the one associated with Luther and the traditional Reformation, the other associated with Erasmus. Both argued a reform of medieval modes of thought, but the latter was more comprehensive than merely a reform and thus at once more modern.

In its original intention and thrust the Reformation was medieval. While the Protestant cause may have been supported by men who had no other concern but to throw off the yoke of the church or free themselves from its financial burden, such was not the intention of the reformers, who wanted to accept the Catholic Church if only that church would grant the seriousness of their concern.

The Renaissance was an intellectual movement, though movement may well be too strong a word, since it never assumed a cohesive empirical form. It was a like-mindedness of aesthetes or intellectuals. It was a *Weltanschauung*, a way of looking at the world, at nature, and man. As such it was profound, searching, and vastly influential; subsequent centuries are unthinkable without its contribution.

The Reformation, on the other hand, was not so much an aesthetic approach to life, but a moral and religious quest. It is telling that the Renaissance, despite its eminent achievements in some areas of human society, notably the arts, did not produce stirring interpreters of life and man. Where it did, as, for example, Erasmus of Rotterdam, the nurture came in large measure from the Christian tradition. It is surely telling that the rich and cultured second half of the fifteenth century in Rome was a time of rather blatant disregard for moral values. The leading exponent of political thought, Machiavelli, may not have been a scoundrel, as has so often been assumed; but he certainly was not a moral thinker either.

Because it was a movement at once moral and practical, the Reformation occupied the heart and minds of men. It was thus able to capture their commitment, cause them to risk life and goods, prompt them to become martyrs. Conviction does not necessarily bespeak truth. However, in this case it does reveal the particular propensity of the movement we call the Reformation. Not that the Protestants numbered only those who stood with the angels: men like Henry VIII or Philipp of Hesse were hardly textbook cases of model moral deportment. But there was a commitment to an ideal that encompassed thought and life as well.

Both Renaissance and Reformation were rebellions, the one primarily artistic and aesthetic, the other moral and religious, against the establishment and the heavy yoke of tradition. Thus a connection between the two does exist and since the Renaissance chronologically preceded the Reformation, one can hardly posit an absolute line of division. But there is no reason to speak of cause and effect.

One might view the Renaissance as that broader era in the history of the West during which a new *Weltanschauung* emerged. This era began before the fifteenth century and lasted beyond the sixteenth; its eminent names like Dante, Michelangelo, Erasmus are cherished words in the world of the heritage of the West. The invention of movable type revolutionized the dissemination of knowledge—if not of wisdom—in the second half of the fifteenth century. Books could be printed more easily and thus more economically. This meant that editions of the works of classical authors, both pagan and Christian, became more widely available. While a book published is not necessarily a book read, there can be little doubt but that the dissemination of the works of the Church Fathers increased considerably during the half-century after the invention of printing. Thus, a different intellectual climate characterized many parts of Europe. The Renaissance did not construct a theological alternative, but it made available the tools that the Protestant reformers subsequently utilized in the formulation of their theologies. In this respect the Reformation is unthinkable without the contribution of the Renaissance.

Still, the Reformation was in a way timeless. If we assume it was not the specifically fifteenth-century theological situation that prompted Luther's protest, the Reformation could have occurred a hundred years earlier for it simply propounded a new formulation of the message of the gospel, such as might have been advanced any time. While it was aided by extraneous factors it was not incisively influenced by them. Indeed, in some ways, the Reformation influenced in its time, the realm of politics no less than that of the arts and letters. Its impact was felt far beyond its own time.

Bibliography

The following bibliography seeks to accomplish a threefold purpose: to present a basic list of important books on the period, primarily in English; to indicate available editions of primary sources (again citing primarily those in English); and, finally, to note the publications available in paperback which are thus most easily accessible. [The last-mentioned are marked with an asterisk.]

I. General Studies
   a. Sources
      *H. J. Hillerbrand. *The Protestant Reformation* (New York, 1967).
      *L. W. Spitz. *The Protestant Reformation* (Englewood Cliffs, N.J., 1966).
      *G. R. Elton. *Renaissance and Reformation: 1300-1648* (New York, 1963).
   b. Studies
      H. J. Grimm. *The Reformation Era* (New York, 1964) [with a valuable bibliography].
      E. L. Leonard. *History of Protestantism*. vol. I (Edinburgh, 1966) [with a valuable bibliography].
      *R. H. Bainton. *The Reformation of the Sixteenth Century* (Boston, 1956).
      *R. H. Bainton. *The Age of the Reformation* (Princeton, 1956).
      *H. Daniel-Rops. *The Protestant Reformation* (London, 1961).
      *O. Chadwick. *The Reformation* (Baltimore, 1964).
      *A. G. Dickens. *Reformation and Society in Sixteenth-Century Europe* (New York, 1966).
      *G. R. Elton. *Reformation Europe 1517-1555* (New York, 1966).
      G. R. Elton, ed. *The Reformation*, vol. II of The New Cambridge Modern History (Cambridge, 1958).
      S. Fischer-Galati. *Ottoman Imperialism and German Protestantism 1521-55* (Cambridge, Massachusetts, 1959).
      H. J. Grimm. *The Reformation in Historical Thought* (New York, 1964) [Service Center for Teachers of History 54].
      *K. Holl. *The Cultural Significance of the Reformation* (New York, 1959).
      *Ph. Hughes. *Popular History of the Reformation* (Garden City, N.Y., 1960).
      *P. Smith. *Age of Reformation*, 2 vols. (New York, 1962).

*L. W. Spitz, ed. *The Reformation—Material or Spiritual?* (Boston, 1962).
*J. Hurstfield. *Reformation Crisis* (New York, 1966).
*J. S. Whale. *The Protestant Tradition* (Cambridge, 1962).
*J. D. Dillenberger and C. Welch. *Protestant Christianity* (New York, 1954).

II. Intellectual Climate

*M. P. Gilmore. *World of Humanism: 1453-1517* (New York, 1962).
*M. Phillips. *Erasmus and the Northern Renaissance* (New York, 1965).
W. K. Ferguson et al. *Facets of the Renaissance* (New York, 1963).
*J. Huizinga. *The Waning of the Middle Ages* (Garden City, N.Y., 1954).
J. Huizinga. *Erasmus and the Age of Reformation* (New York, 1957).
J. C. Olin, ed. *Desiderius Erasmus. Christian Humanism and the Reformation* (New York, 1965).
E. Harbison. *The Christian Scholar in the Age of the Reformation* (New York, 1961).
G. Mattingly. *Renaissance Diplomacy* (New York, 1955).
L. W. Spitz. *The Religious Renaissance of the German Humanists* (Cambridge, Mass., 1963).
*R. W. Chambers. *Thomas More* (Ann Arbor, Mich., 1958).
A. R. Hall. *The Scientific Revolution* (London, 1954).
J. H. Parry. *Europe and the Wider World, 1415-1715* (London, 1949).

III. Germany and Luther

a. Sources

Luther's Works. American Edition. J. J. Pelikan and H. T. Lehmann, eds. (St. Louis-Philadelphia, 1955 ff.) [to comprise fifty-five volumes].
Martin Luther. *Lectures on Romans.* Tr. and ed. by W. Pauck. Vol. XV of The Library of Christian Classics (Philadelphia, 1961).
*Martin Luther. *Three Treatises* (Philadelphia, 1960).
*J. Dillenberger, ed. *Martin Luther: Selections from His Writings* (Chicago, 1961).

b. Studies

H. Holborn. *A History of Modern Germany*, vol. I. The Reformation (New York, 1959).
*H. Holborn. *Ulrich Von Hutten and the German Reformation* (New York, 1965).
*Heinrich Bornkamm. *Luther's Doctrine of the Two Kingdoms* (Philadelphia, 1966).
*E. G. Rupp. *Luther's Progress to the Diet of Worms* (New York, 1964).
*H. Bornkamm. *Luther's World of Thought* (St. Louis, 1966).
*C. Bergendoff. *Olavus Petri and the Ecclesiastical Transformation of Sweden* (Philadelphia, 1965).

IV. England

a. Sources

The Parker Society Publications, 55 vols. (Cambridge, 1843-1855) [contain the writings of the eminent Anglican divines of the sixteenth century].
H. Gee and W. J. Hardy. *Documents Illustrative of English Church History* (London, 1914).

P. L. Hughes and J. F. Larkin, eds. *The Early Tudors (1485-1553)*. Tudor Proclamations, vol. 1. (New Haven, 1964).

C. H. Williams, ed. *English Historical Documents*. Vol. V. 1485-1558 (New York, 1967).

W. C. Dickinson, ed. John Knox. *History of the Reformation in Scotland*. 2 vols. (London, 1950).

*C. S. Meyer. *Cranmer's Selected Writings* (London, 1961).

b. Studies

R. Walcott. *The Tudor-Stuart Period of English History: A Review of Changing Interpretations* (New York, 1964) [Service Center for Teachers of History].

G. R. Elton. *England under the Tudors* (London, 1954).

L. B. Smith et al. *This Realm of England 1399-1688*. History of England, vol. II. (Boston, 1966).

*G. R. Elton. *Tudor Revolution in Government* (Cambridge, 1959).

*F. M. Powicke. *The Reformation in England* (London, 1961).

*G. Constant. *The Reformation in England: The English Schism and Henry VIII, 1509-1547* (New York, 1966).

P. Hughes. *The Reformation in England*. 3 vols. (New York, 1950-1954).

*A. G. Dickens. *The English Reformation* (New York, 1964).

G. Mattingly. *Catherine of Aragon* (New York, 1960).

E. G. Rupp. *Studies in the Making of the English Protestant Tradition* (Cambridge, 1949).

E. G. Rupp. *Six Makers of English Religion, 1500-1700* (New York, 1957).

*J. Ridley. *Thomas Cranmer* (New York, 1966).

*W. Haller. *The Rise of Puritanism* (New York, 1957).

*M. M. Knappen. *Tudor Puritanism* (Chicago, 1939; Gloucester, Mass., 1963).

P. Hughes. *Rome and the Counter-Reformation in England* (London, 1942).

V. Radical Protestantism

a. Sources

G. H. Williams and A. M. Mergal, eds. *Spiritual and Anabaptist Writers*. Vol. XXV of the Library of Christian Classics (Philadelphia, 1957).

The Complete Works of Menno Simons (c. 1496-1561). Tr. by L. Verduin and ed. by J. C. Wenger (Scottdale, Penn'a., 1956).

b. Studies

H. S. Bender. *Conrad Grebel* (Goshen, Ind., 1950).

R. Friedmann. *Hutterite Studies* (Goshen, Ind., 1961).

*Fr. Blanke. *Brothers in Christ* (Scottdale, Penn'a., 1961).

*F. H. Littell. *The Origins of Sectarian Protestantism* (New York, 1964).

The Mennonite Encyclopedia, 4 vols. (Scottdale, Penn'a., 1955 ff.).

*R. H. Bainton. *The Travail of Religious Liberty* (New York, 1958).

G. H. Williams. *The Radical Reformation* (Philadelphia, 1962).

*R. H. Bainton: *Hunted Heretic: The Life and Death of Michael Servetus 1511-1553* (Boston, 1960).

VI. Catholic Reform and Reaction
   a. Sources
      H. J. Schroeder, ed. *Canons and Decrees of the Council of Trent* (St. Louis, 1950).
      The Spiritual Exercises of Saint Ignatius (New York, 1963).
      Letters of St. Ignatius of Loyola. Selected and transl. by W. J. Young (Chicago, 1959).
      St. Ignatius of Loyola. *St. Ignatius' Own Story* (Chicago, 1950).
   b. Studies
      L. v. Pastor. *History of the Popes.* Vols. VIII-XV (London, 1908-28).
      P. Janelle. *The Catholic Reformation* (Milwaukee, 1949).
      *J. Brodrick. *The Origins of the Jesuits* (Garden City, N.Y., 1960).
      J. Brodrick. *The Progress of the Jesuits* (New York, 1947).
      H. Jedin. *History of the Council of Trent.* 2 vols. (London, 1957-61).
      *H. Daniel-Rops. *The Catholic Reformation* (New York, 1962).
VII. Outstanding Figures
      *K. Brandi. *The Emperor Charles V* (London, 1966).
      *G. R. Elton. *Henry VIII: An Essay in Revision* (London, 1962).
      L. v. Matt. *St. Ignatius of Loyola* (Chicago, 1956; New York, 1963).
      *R. H. Bainton. *Here I Stand* (New York, 1952).
      *E. Erikson. *Young Man Luther: A Study in Psychoanalysis and History* (New York, 1962).
      *A. F. Pollard. *Henry VIII* (New York, 1966).
      J. Brodrick. *St. Ignatius Loyola: The Pilgrim Years* (New York, 1956).
      B. Gerrish, ed. *Reformers in Profile* (Philadelphia, 1967).
      *M. Weber. *The Protestant Ethic and the Spirit of Capitalism* (New York, 1958).
      K. Samuelssen. *Religion and Economic Action* (New York, 1961).
      J. J. Scarisbrick. *Henry VIII* (London, 1968).

Index

PRINTED IN U.S.A.